BARRON'S BOOK NOTES

ALAN PATON'S

Cry, the Beloved Country

BARRON'S BOOK NOTES

ALAN PATON'S

Cry, the Beloved Country

BY

Rose Sallberg Kam

SERIES COORDINATOR

Murray Bromberg
Principal, Wang High School of Queens
Holliswood, New York

BARRON'S EDUCATIONAL SERIES, INC.
Woodbury, New York • London • Toronto • Sydney

ACKNOWLEDGMENTS

Our thanks to Milton Katz and Julius Liebb for their contribution to the Book Notes series.

All inquiries should be addressed to:
Barron's Educational Series, Inc.
113 Crossways Park Drive
Woodbury, New York 11797

Library of Congress Catalog Card No. 85-1353

International Standard Book No. 0-8120-3507-0

Library of Congress Cataloging in Publication Data

Kam, Rose.
   Alan Paton's Cry, the beloved country.

   (Barron's book notes)
   Bibliography: p.105
   Summary: A guide to reading "Cry, the Beloved Country"
with a critical and appreciative mind. Includes
background on the author's life and times, sample tests,
term paper suggestions, and a reading list.
   1. Paton, Alan, Cry, the beloved country.
[1. Paton, Alan, Cry, the beloved country. 2. South
African literature (English)—History and criticism]
I. Title. II. Series.
PR9369.3.P37C735   1985   823   85-1333
ISBN 0-8120-3507-0

PRINTED IN THE UNITED STATES OF AMERICA

567   550   987654321

CONTENTS

ADVISORY BOARD

HOW TO USE THIS BOOK

You have to know how to approach literature in order to get the most out of it. This *Barron's Book Notes* volume follows a plan based on methods used by some of the best students to read a work of literature.

Begin with the guide's section on the author's life and times. As you read, try to form a clear picture of the author's personality, circumstances, and motives for writing the work. This background usually will make it easier for you to hear the author's tone of voice, and follow where the author is heading.

Then go over the rest of the introductory material—such sections as those on the plot, characters, setting, themes, and style of the work. Underline, or write down in your notebook, particular things to watch for, such as contrasts between characters and repeated literary devices. At this point, you may want to develop a system of symbols to use in marking your text as you read. (Of course, you should only mark up a book you own, not one that belongs to another person or a school.) Perhaps you will want to use a different letter for each character's name, a different number for each major theme of the book, a different color for each important symbol or literary device. Be prepared to mark up the pages of your book as you read. Put your marks in the margins so you can find them again easily.

Now comes the moment you've been waiting for—the time to start reading the work of literature. You may want to put aside your *Barron's Book Notes* volume until you've read the work all the way through. Or you may want to alternate, reading the *Book Notes* analysis of each section as soon as you have finished reading the corresponding part of the original. Before you move on, reread crucial passages you don't fully understand. (Don't take this guide's analysis for granted—make up your own mind as to what the work means.)

Once you've finished the whole work of literature, you may want to review it right away, so you can firm up your ideas about what it means. You may want to leaf through the book concentrating on passages you marked in reference to one character or one theme. This is also a good time to reread the *Book Notes* introductory material, which pulls together insights on specific topics.

When it comes time to prepare for a test or to write a paper, you'll already have formed ideas about the work. You'll be able to go back through it, refreshing your memory as to the author's exact words and perspective, so that you can support your opinions with evidence drawn straight from the work. Patterns will emerge, and ideas will fall into place; your essay question or term paper will almost write itself. Give yourself a dry run with one of the sample tests in the guide. These tests present both multiple-choice and essay questions. An accompanying section gives answers to the multiple-choice questions as well as suggestions for writing the essays. If you have to select a term paper topic, you may choose one from the list of suggestions in this book. This guide also provides you with a reading list, to help you when you start research for a term paper, and a selection of provocative comments by critics, to spark your thinking before you write.

THE AUTHOR
AND HIS TIMES

Every moviegoer is familiar with the scene. There is a bundle of dynamite waiting menacingly. A match is struck and touched to the end of the long fuse. Slowly the flame eats its way along the wire. Paralyzed with fear, you follow its progress toward the explosives.

Attempts have been made to stop the blast but to no avail. In a few moments, so to speak, the earth will be rocked by the powerful detonation, and the world will be staggered by the statistics of the dead and dying.

By the time you are reading this guide to *Cry, The Beloved Country* the catastrophe may have already taken place, for the above description applies to the volatile Republic of South Africa. There, the long time tensions between blacks and whites have been expected to result in a massive upheaval, accompanied by great pain and bloodshed. If the blacks, the majority group in South Africa, cannot gain control of their country through an orderly process, we may yet see the dynamite, the symbol of their latent power, explode in a deafening roar.

One person who has been striving mightily to prevent the horror is Alan Paton, the author of *Cry, the Beloved Country*. He has spoken out against *apartheid*, his country's policy of racial segregation with the minority group of whites in control. Using his talent as a writer, Paton has protested against the demeaning policy of apartheid. Through his articles and stories he has worked to cut the fuse before the dynamite is reached. As you learn about Paton's life, you will come to understand why he has waged his passionate crusade against racial prejudice and its ugly by-products.

Let's go back to a September afternoon in 1946 when the homesick Alan Paton returned to his hotel room in Norway and wrote these lines:

> There is a lovely road that runs from Ixopo into the hills. These hills are grass-covered and rolling, and they are lovely beyond any singing of it.

As the principal of a reform school in South Africa, he was studying prisons for the young in Norway, Sweden, Canada, and the United States. The words he wrote about the hills of his home province of Natal released a torrent of thoughts for the lonely Paton. He thought about his country, its people, and the causes of the high crime rate among young blacks in South Africa. By the time he reached San Francisco in early 1947, he had completed the manuscript of *Cry, the Beloved Country*. As recently as 1982, Paton still spoke of the 1948 publication of *Cry, the Beloved Country* as the central event of his life.

Like Arthur Jarvis in this famous novel, Paton came from an English-speaking family in the South African province of Natal. He was born in Pietermaritzburg on January 11, 1903. His mother was a third-generation South African of English descent. His father was a Scot who had come to South Africa as a civil servant just before the South African (or Boer) War (1899–1902).

Paton's childhood came during a time of promise. The British, who were relatively forward-looking on racial matters, had won the South African War, a bloody conflict with the Boers. (Boers, or Afrikaners, are descended from settlers of mainly Dutch, French Huguenot, and German descent. They speak the Afrikaans language, which is derived largely from Dutch.) In 1910 the British linked Natal, Transvaal, Cape, and the Orange Free State to form the self-governing Union of South Africa.

Paton's parents held comparatively liberal political views. They also taught their children that Afrikaners had a right to preserve their own culture. Paton was educated at a high school for white boys, Maritzburg College in Pietermaritzburg, and then Natal University College, where he majored in math and physics. At the university college he not only gained an education, but also broadened his understanding of Afrikaners, blacks, Coloureds (as persons of mixed ancestry are called by the government of South Africa), and Indians. He was especially active in the Student Christian Association, a society dear to Paton's hero, the South African political leader Jan Hofmeyr. Unlike Paton, Hofmyer was of Boer descent, but he urged his fellow Boers to abandon bitter memories and to work for the good of all South Africans.

As a young man Paton also learned to speak both Afrikaans and Zulu, like Arthur Jarvis in *Cry, the Beloved Country*. In fact, Paton might be taken as a model for Arthur—a man with strong Christian beliefs who gradually decides he wants to devote his life to improving race relations in his country.

In 1925 Paton began teaching at the white high

school in Ixopo. (His love of the area shows in *Cry, the Beloved Country*, from the first two sentences on.) While teaching in Ixopo, Paton met Doris Olive Francis, a third-generation South African whose husband was ill with tuberculosis. In 1928, three years after her husband died, she and Paton were married. The strong attachment to the Anglican Church that Paton developed in this period in his life shows in *Cry, the Beloved Country*—all the major characters are Anglican.

The newly married couple moved to Pietermaritzburg so that Paton could take a more promising job at his old high school. Six years later he suffered a severe attack of typhoid and was hospitalized for more than two months. During his recuperation he decided he didn't want to spend the rest of his life teaching the sons of the rich. By that time Jan Hofmeyr was Minister of Education, so Paton asked his advice. Hofmeyr and the Prime Minister, Jan Christiaan Smuts, had just gotten three reformatories for delinquents under age 21 transferred from the justice department to the ministry of education. Hofmeyr advised his friend to apply for the job of warden at all three places.

Paton did apply, despite his lack of experience in the criminal justice system, and was appointed warden of Diepkloof Reformatory for African Juvenile Delinquents, a grim place outside Johannesburg enclosed by a barbed-wire stockade. Even Hofmeyr said, "It is hard to know what can be done with it," but Paton was excited—at the age of 32 he'd been given a prison to turn into a school. Like the young white man from the reformatory in *Cry, the Beloved Country*, he felt he had a chance to change the lives of young blacks. The job lasted from 1935 to 1948, a period during which Paton also wrote articles like those in Arthur Jarvis' desk drawer. In fact, one of Paton's essays—"Who Is Really to Blame for the Crime Wave in South Africa?" (*The Forum*, December 15, 1945)—presents the themes of the novel as well as those of Arthur's paper in Chapter 20 on the causes of crime among young blacks.

Given a free hand, Paton transformed Diepkloof. It held 400 boys (later more than 600), mostly blacks of the Xhosa ethnic group. He was appalled at the joyless atmosphere, and, every morning, at the stench. After supper and a full workday on the prison farm, the boys were locked up for 14 hours. From 5:00 P.M. to 7:00 A.M. they used buckets in their cells as latrines. Paton immediately began opening cell blocks till 9:00 P.M., starting with those of the younger boys, so they could use the prison bathrooms till then. He also let the boys romp, sing, and paint pictures on the whitewashed walls. By the time he was opening all the cell blocks, he had also had more bathrooms built. His changes brought some joy to the place, eliminated the morning stink, and also ended the typhoid outbreaks that had previously caused many deaths.

When World War II broke out in 1939, Paton tried to enlist in the South African army, but education officials considered him too valuable to let go. By the time the war ended in 1945, Paton was considered an authority on criminal rehabilitation, but he wondered how other countries ran penal institutions for the young. To find out, he financed an eight-month study trip. He didn't leave home with the intention of writing a novel while traveling. What started him off, that September afternoon in Norway, was a tour of the cathedral of Trondheim. The beauty of its famous rose window made him yearn to write about his beautiful homeland and its people. As Paton explains in an Author's Note to *Cry, the Beloved Country*, it was in San Francisco that friends read his manuscript and started contacting publishers. The book was first published in New York in early 1948.

The novel sold well both in North America and in Great Britain. It was soon translated into some 20 languages, and made into a film in England (1952) and a musical in the United States (*Lost in the Stars*, 1949, script by the playwright Maxwell Anderson and music by the German-American composer Kurt Weill). The South African edition, dedicated to Jan Hofmeyr, came out three months before Hofmeyr's death at age 54 in December 1948. Book sales in South Africa were second only to those of the Bible, and Paton became famous.

Critic James Stern in the *New Republic* called it "one of the best novels of our time." And Orville Prescott, *The New York Times* book reviewer, wrote in the *Yale Review* that Paton's novel was "the finest I have ever read about the tragic plight of black-skinned people in a white man's world."

Another event of importance to the Patons also occurred in 1948—the coming to power of the Nationalist Party, pledged to separation of the races in every sphere of life. At Diepkloof the Patons had ignored people's color in forming friendships, and they could not endure the new government's opposition to interracial association. With the success of his novel making Paton influential, he ultimately became a full-time writer and spokesman against injustice. Years later, in *For You Departed*, he wrote about the novel and that time period: "It is a song of love for one's far distant country. . . . It is a story of the beauty and terror of human life. . . . Just how good it is, I do not know and do not care. All I know is that it changed our lives. It opened the doors of the world to us, and we went through."

In 1953 the Liberal Association of South Africa (later the Liberal Party) was formed, and Paton was named its first national chairman. For the next 15 years Paton's life was dominated by activities of the racially mixed party, by writing plays for multiracial casts and audiences, and by political writing and speaking. One play, *Mkhumbane*, drew packed houses in Durban City Hall in 1960—a time of peaceful black protest against apartheid at Sharpeville and Cape Town that was dealt with extremely harshly by the government.

For his work on behalf of the people of South Africa and against the evils of apartheid, Paton has received international recognition. In 1960, the noted American poet Archibald MacLeish toasted Alan Paton when the South African received the Freedom Award from Freedom House:

> To live at the center of the contemporary maelstrom; to see it for what it is and to challenge the passions of those who struggle in it beside him with the voice of reason—with the enduring reasons of love; to offer the quiet sanity of the heart in a city yammering with the crazy slogans of fear; to do all this at the cost of tranquility and the risk of harm, as a service to a government which does not know its needs is to deserve more of history than we can give to Alan Paton.

Until shortly before her death in 1967, Paton's

wife typed all of his work, including the novel *Too Late the Phalarope* (1953), the story collection *Tales from a Troubled Land* (1961), and the biography *Hofmeyr* (1964). Since her death, Paton's best-known work includes *For You Departed* (1969), a memoir dedicated to her, and *The Long View* (1968), a collection of articles from a Liberal Party publication. More recent is his novel set in the 1950s, *Ah, But Your Land is Beautiful* (1981)—the title is a phrase borrowed from bewildered tourists who give up trying to understand South African politics.

All of Paton's books show his love of his country and his compassion for all South Africans. He still hopes that violence there will end, that the dynamite will never be ignited, and that the views that will prevail will be like those of Arthur Jarvis and Msimangu in *Cry, the Beloved Country*.

THE NOVEL

The Plot

It's 1946, and drought is eroding parts of Natal, a province of the Union of South Africa. Uplands near the village of Ndotsheni are still fertile, but the soil is depleted in lowlands reserved for blacks of the once powerful Zulu nation. The Reverend Stephen Kumalo is worried. With crops too sparse to feed everyone, young people have been going off to Johannesburg. Very few ever return. One of those gone is Sibeko's daughter who accompanied her white mistress, Miss Smith, to a Johannesburg suburb. Others are members of the parson's own family. Kumalo's brother John has been in Johannesburg ten years; his sister Gertrude took her baby and left to find her husband two or three years back; and his son Absalom has been gone for more than a year. Kumalo fears that strict Zulu moral traditions, based on family unity, may be breaking down completely.

One day Kumalo hears from the Reverend Theophilus Msimangu, a Zulu and an Anglican priest like himself. Msimangu writes that Kumalo must come to Johannesburg immediately because Gertrude is ill. Once Kumalo quits worrying about the expense, he enjoys the trip. He gawks without embarrassment at more trains, stations, people, and streets than he had ever imagined. In Johannesburg, however, his delight fades. A young black man tricks him out of some money, and then Msimangu tells him Gertrude isn't physically sick—she's a prostitute.

The next day, though, after many tears, Gertrude agrees to give up prostitution. She and her little boy move to Kumalo's rooming house until he is ready to take them back to Ndotsheni. His good spirits restored, Kumalo expects equally successful reunions with his brother and his son. It sounds easy. Absalom's best friend is John's son, Matthew, and Msimangu says that everyone knows John Kumalo. He owns a prosperous shop and gives rousing speeches on such issues as fair wages for black workers. But Stephen Kumalo is bitterly disappointed with John, who has left the Anglican Church. He lives with a woman who isn't his wife and doesn't even know where his own son is— much less Absalom. Kumalo reluctantly acknowledges that his brother will never return to Ndotsheni, but he still hopes that his own son Absalom will.

With Msimangu as his guide, Kumalo finds a factory John mentioned. But Absalom no longer works there. It also turns out that he has moved from the address a man at the factory provides, and from the next, too. Each new address is in a worse neighborhood. Kumalo tries to ignore a conclusion he is reaching, but he has seen and heard too much. The wealth of white districts and the poverty and lack of work in black ones make crime all too attractive to any idle boy—even *his* son. It's almost a relief when he and Msimangu (close friends by then) learn at last that Absalom is in reform school for burglary. But their relief fades. Officials have released him to marry a girl he made pregnant, and she hasn't seen him for days.

That evening, headlines further alarm Kumalo. Three young blacks have killed a prominent white man, a spokesman for social reform named Arthur

Jarvis. Hundreds of boys might have killed him, but Kumalo is sick with fear that Absalom is one of the three. A thin connection feeds his fear. Arthur was the son of James Jarvis of High Place above Ndotsheni, and Kumalo remembers Arthur as a cheerful little boy who used to come into the village.

Tired and downhearted, Kumalo accepts Msimangu's invitation to a day of rest and prayer outside Johannesburg. He gains some inner peace, and glimpses the possibility of better schooling in his village—education in farming methods that might improve the land enough to keep young people home, or at least provision of kinds of knowledge that would help them adapt to city life.

Meanwhile the police, spurred on by public outrage, have worked quickly. In a few days they've arrested Absalom, Matthew, and another boy—and Absalom has confessed that he pulled the trigger. Still, Kumalo is relieved that Absalom did not fire deliberately, and that he repents and plans to tell the entire truth. When his brother John hires a lawyer to defend Matthew by denying Absalom's story, Kumalo is stunned. John has betrayed the most basic Zulu value—family loyalty.

During the trial, whites and blacks alike fill the segregated courtroom. James Jarvis, Arthur's father, doesn't notice Kumalo, but Kumalo notices him. He wonders how he will ever be able to face Jarvis. Meanwhile Jarvis has been studying his son's speeches and articles. Arthur had worked toward correcting wrongs that whites had committed against blacks, and Jarvis begins to want to carry on his son's ideas. But he wonders what, exactly, he should do.

One day court is not in session. The Jarvises visit

their niece, Barbara Smith, and Kumalo decides to keep his promise to look for Sibeko's daughter. He knocks on the Smiths' door in a Johannesburg suburb, and Jarvis answers. Kumalo is shocked speechless and needs time to recover enough to conduct his errand. Jarvis gradually realizes that Kumalo is shaking with fear, and recognizes him as the parson from Ndotsheni. Genuinely concerned, he asks why Kumalo is so afraid. Kumalo finally manages to say the painful words, "It was my son that killed your son." Jarvis in turn is shocked, but he is understanding. Instead of blaming Kumalo for his son's actions, he sees him as a father like himself—a man full of grief over a son.

The trial ends in acquittal for Matthew and the other boy, but Absalom is sentenced to hang in Pretoria a few weeks later. He is allowed to marry his girlfriend, and Kumalo promises to take her home so the child can be born and raised in Ndotsheni. Kumalo attempts a reconciliation with John, but they only quarrel, and Kumalo has no further reason to stay in Johannesburg. Gertrude, meanwhile, has had second thoughts about quiet village life. Leaving her little boy in the care of Absalom's wife, she sneaks off in the night. The others travel to Ndotsheni without her. On their way, Kumalo worries. Will his people take back a parson with relatives like Gertrude and Absalom? But the villagers welcome him warmly, and Mrs. Kumalo greets Absalom's wife and Gertrude's boy as her own children.

Later in the week Kumalo goes to the tribal chief and the schoolmaster, but they don't understand his dreams for the future. Nothing changes until the day Arthur's young son, James Jarvis' grandson, rides up to Kumalo's house. When Kumalo says that he can't give the boy the cold milk he asks for, the boy comes to understand how desperately the village children need milk. Then he simply goes and has his grandfather send some. The action seems to inspire Jarvis. He provides not just milk, but also the more lasting help of a new dam and advice from an agricultural expert. Kumalo encourages the willing villagers to try the new ways, and spurs on the reluctant ones.

Jarvis and Kumalo seldom actually talk, but when they do—as they do one night on the mountain where Kumalo has gone to keep watch before and during Absalom's execution—their understanding is complete. Neither the Kumalo nor the Jarvis family can be restored, and neither can the old Zulu ways. But in Ndotsheni, at least, a white man and a black man are working together to restore the land they love.

The Characters

Some characters in *Cry, the Beloved Country*—even some major characters—are more types than individuals. That is, they stand for kinds of people, and you see only one side of their personalities. Some minor characters are also presented as types. They are not given names. Instead, they are always introduced by the same phrase—for example, "the young white man from the reformatory."

MAJOR CHARACTERS
Reverend Stephen Kumalo
Kumalo is the Zulu pastor of St. Mark's Church of Ndotsheni, a village near the town of Ixopo in the

province of Natal. An American skimming this novel might at first see Kumalo as an "Uncle Tom." He seems almost too respectful of whites and not very assertive about the needs and rights of his own people. But Kumalo is far more complex than that. Some readers see Kumalo as a basically good man who achieves a kind of saintliness because of his experiences in the novel. Whatever your personal interpretation is, Kumalo is the most fully developed character—perhaps the only fully developed character—in the novel.

He does begin as a fairly innocent "country boy," despite being 60 years old and educated enough to serve as a village parson. As you first meet him, he is somewhat timid, yet a little vain about his status as pastor. He and his wife are poor, but their strong love of family is clearly shown by their willingness to spend their savings on the journey to Johannesburg.

In Johannesburg, city ways bewilder Kumalo at first. He is even cheated out of some money as soon as he arrives. But he is able to learn, and can eventually get around the city by himself. You see that he is a kind man when he buys his sister and her child new clothes. He is tenacious, too. He does not easily accept defeat in his search for his son, and even opposes his friend Msimangu who advises him against accepting his son's pregnant girl. He's not totally angelic, however. When Kumalo sees people close to him violating the strict moral code they've been taught, anger consumes him and he speaks out cruelly. He quickly repents, however, and begs forgiveness.

Almost without noticing it, he begins to see the drought and the breakup of families in his own village in a new light. He begins to understand that whites have caused many of the social and economic problems of blacks. In his own life, however, he finds it difficult to change lifetime habits and speak up to white men he respects, like his bishop or James Jarvis.

Kumalo suffers deeply. By the end of the novel he has lost a brother, a sister, and a son. But he has gained a daughter-in-law, a nephew, and a grandchild as yet unborn. Once, when much younger, he had considered taking a job that would pay better than the priesthood. But suffering ennobles him. He grows into every bit as much a man of God as his friends Msimangu and Father Vincent. Instead of becoming a bitter old man, he acquires the vision to propose improvements for the good of his village.

Reverend Theophilus Msimangu

Msimangu is an Anglican priest assigned to the Mission House in Sophiatown, a district of Johannesburg. His first name means "one who loves God." Msimangu seems better educated than Kumalo, and speaks Afrikaans as well as Zulu and English. He is a powerful preacher and a sophisticated, knowledgeable man. He is also sensitive and is deeply affected by the injustices suffered by blacks. He considers love the only force strong enough to bring whites and blacks together. Msimangu calls Kumalo to Johannesburg because of Gertrude, takes him to Gertrude and to John Kumalo, and then helps him search for Absalom. Sometimes disillusionment sets off his temper. For example, when Kumalo wants to take in Absalom's girl, Msimangu angrily dismisses her as a slut who is unlikely to change. Like Kumalo, however, Msimangu quickly regrets his words and asks forgiveness. He ultimately gives Kumalo all his savings and enters a monastery. You are not told why. What is your thinking on the matter? Perhaps he believes a priest doesn't belong in politics, or perhaps he is simply following his own deep attraction to the spiritual life.

Gertrude Kumalo

Kumalo's sister Gertrude is young enough to be his daughter. When her husband, a miner, disappeared in Johannesburg, she took their baby and left to look for him. She never found him, but quickly embraced the freedom of the city even though she could earn her way only by prostitution, gambling, and the making and selling of bad liquor. It's possible that for dramatic reasons, Paton decided to have Gertrude drift into prostitution. With the knowledge that you have gained from reading *Cry, the Beloved Country*, what other alternatives were there? If Paton had depicted Gertrude solely as a cook in a shabby restaurant would that have been just as effective for his purposes?

When Kumalo confronts her with the shame she has brought on the family, she seems to repent. But in the end she knows that she cannot possibly go back to the restrictions of village life. She gives her little boy to Absalom's new wife and disappears again into Johannesburg. Gertrude is more a type than a complex individual. She is so changed by city life that she cannot return to traditional Zulu values.

John Kumalo

Kumalo's brother John is a carpenter who moved to Johannesburg and became prosperous. He has

left the church, his wife Esther has left him for
being unfaithful to her, and he lives with a woman
he hasn't married. A fat, bull-necked man, he is a
prominent speaker whose powerful voice could
move thousands of people to action. Yet he always
stops short of inciting a riot. He fears being arrested and losing his comfortable life. When his
son Matthew is arrested with Absalom on suspi-
cion of murder, he hires a crooked lawyer to get
his son acquitted. John's narrow action on behalf
of his son alone, shocks Stephen Kumalo. (You
might want to consider other ways John could have
acted.) After the trial John plans to keep a better
eye on Matthew, but it is doubtful that his own
moral standards will inspire his son. He, too, is
somewhat of a type character, a Zulu man changed
by the city, but he emerges as a more complex
individual than Gertrude.

Absalom Kumalo

Absalom's name recalls the rebellious son of King
David in the Bible. He turns against the ideals of
his father when he drifts into thievery—a life which
puts him in a prison school. He does well there,
but when he is released to marry his pregnant girlfriend, he drifts back to crime. Eventually he fires
a gun during a robbery and kills an important white
man, Arthur Jarvis. He is tried, and sentenced to
death. He is meek and repentant in captivity and
you see the young man he might have become. He
dies wishing that he could start over. He is a case
study of a black youth in the middle—he could
have gone either way, but was drawn into a life of
crime by social conditions he neither caused nor
understood. Of course, there were thousands of
young blacks like Absalom Kumalo who didn't be-

come criminals at that time regardless of social conditions. Should Alan Paton have dealt with them here?

Matthew Kumalo

The son of John Kumalo, Matthew can be seen as an outright thief and liar who laughs at his cousin for confessing to breaking into the home of Arthur Jarvis and to firing the shot that killed him. The lawyer hired by his father wins his acquittal, although he and the third boy, Johannes Pafuri, are under investigation for other crimes. While Matthew is presented in a bad light, you should try to understand the forces that worked against him. Was he born a thief and a liar? Is this the situation of a "bad seed," an incorrigible youth, or is the interpretation of Matthew's character a far more complex matter?

Arthur Jarvis

Born and raised near Ndotsheni, Arthur Jarvis is a well-educated man who becomes so dedicated to social reform that he is willing to abandon a successful business to spread his beliefs. In many ways he is a surrogate (or stand-in) for Paton and his views. He is so strong an advocate of blacks as almost to be a savior, and it is ironic that he should be killed by blacks. Some readers see him as a Christ figure. In what ways might this be true?

James Jarvis

James Jarvis is Arthur Jarvis's father, the prosperous owner of High Place near Ndotsheni. He is a devoted husband, a kind, considerate man, and an employer whose workers love him. He is, however, blind to social injustice until the murder. The crime and his reading of his son's papers destroy his orderly world. He comes to believe that he must do more than live a decent personal life—that he must help rebuild what other white men have destroyed. He donates a large sum of money to a boys' club founded by his son and John Harrison, and joins with Kumalo to begin reforms in Ndotsheni.

Mrs. Lithebe

Mrs. Lithebe is a childless widow who rents Kumalo a room in Sophiatown. She doesn't need the rent money, but is so impressed with Kumalo that she takes in Gertrude and her son, as well as Absalom's girlfriend, for Kumalo's sake. Mrs. Lithebe finds answers to life's problems in religion and strict morals. She likes Gertrude, but instructs Absalom's girlfriend to avoid her influence. She serves as the mother the girl never had.

MINOR CHARACTERS

Mrs. Stephen Kumalo

Stephen Kumalo's wife is a Zulu woman who bears whatever comes her way. She is forceful once a decision is made, and staunchly supports Kumalo. Warm-hearted, she welcomes Absalom's wife and Gertrude's son as her own children.

Wife of Mpanza

She is a woman of Ndotsheni whose son was so excited by Johannesburg that he stepped into the path of a large truck. In a way, the boy's excitement prepares us for Kumalo's reactions to Johannesburg.

The Man Who Carried The Bags
He is a Zulu friend and advisor of Kumalo's, who helps him see that people do not blame him for his relatives' behavior. He takes Kumalo to the train and meets him when he returns. A willing go-between, he asks Kumalo to locate the daughter of Sibeko in the Johannesburg suburb of Springs. He is so happy working for James Jarvis that he says he would die if Jarvis asked it.

Mr. Mafolo
Mr. Mafolo is an Anglican businessman who rescues Kumalo and takes him to Msimangu on his first night in Johannesburg.

Father Vincent
Father Vincent is a rosy-cheeked, good-natured priest from England assigned to the Mission House with Msimangu. He helps persuade a white lawyer, Mr. Carmichael, to take Absalom's case.

Dubula
A black man described as the heart and soul of protest in Johannesburg. Because he is incorruptible, government officials consider him dangerous. He organizes the bus boycott and inspires the building of Shanty Town.

The Young White Man
from the Reformatory
He is dedicated to helping delinquents become good citizens. He takes Absalom's return to crime as a

personal failure and goes out of his way to help Kumalo. He gives him rides, urges him to get a lawyer for Absalom, keeps him informed, and comforts him. Like Arthur, he represents those whites who are working to build a better future.

The Pregnant Girl
She is the girl who is pregnant with Absalom's child. An orphan, she has survived by living with any man who wants her. At Mrs. Lithebe's house she is at first attracted to Gertrude's ways, but changes under the influence of Kumalo and Mrs. Lithebe. She agrees to raise Gertrude's son if Gertrude should leave, marries Absalom so that her own baby will be legitimate, and goes back to Ndotsheni with Kumalo. She and her unborn child also represent hope for the future.

Johannes Pafuri
He is arrested with Absalom and Matthew Kumalo for the killing of Arthur Jarvis. Like Matthew, he is acquitted.

John Harrison
He is the brother of Mary Jarvis, Arthur's wife. He idolized Arthur Jarvis and helped him establish the African Boys' Club in Claremont. He takes the Jarvises to his parents' house during their stay in Johannesburg.

Mr. Harrison
He is John Harrison's father, a man who respected but thoroughly disagreed with Arthur Jarvis. He explains Afrikaner or Nationalist positions to James Jarvis after Arthur's funeral.

The Small White Boy

He is Arthur's 9-year-old son. He visits High Place and Ndotsheni after Arthur's death, and asks Kumalo to teach him Zulu. In their conversations, he quickly grasps the poverty of Kumalo's people. He asks his grandfather to send milk for sick children, and that action begins a series of projects shared by Kumalo and James Jarvis. The boy is an angelic figure whose inner goodness offers hope for the future.

The Chief

He is the ineffective, almost comical head of Kumalo's tribe. The pitiful way he tries to help set stakes for the dam site makes Stephen Kumalo realize his brother John was right about one thing— the tribe needs a different kind of leadership.

Other Elements

SETTING

The settings in *Cry, the Beloved Country* are more than just backdrops or pictures of the country Paton loves. They are also symbols or metaphors for the themes and events of the novel. Part of your interpretation of the novel will probably be based on how you feel about the major settings, rural Natal and urban Johannesburg.

Paton knew the area around Ndotsheni well. He taught school there when he was a young man. It is here that most of the main characters in the novel were born, and it is to here they return. It is here that hope for the next generation arises. Yet, even if this area of rural Natal is a place of rebirth, it also reflects the divisions in South African society. The uplands, reserved for whites, are lush, green, and fertile. The valley below, reserved for blacks, is dry and eroded. When it rains, the reddened earth seems to flow with blood—a powerful symbol of the losses white rule and mismanagement have brought to the black population.

Johannesburg is very different. It is big, bright, and overwhelming. It has considerable attraction for many of the characters in the novel.

Like the area around Ndotsheni, Johannesburg shows us the many divisions between blacks and whites. There are the well-kept white areas and the shabby black sections of town. But Paton does more with Johannesburg than take the reader on a tour. Take a look at the neighborhoods Kumalo visits while searching for Absalom. Would the story be as effective if Paton had rearranged the order in which they are visited? Are these parts of town picked at random or do they tell us in a symbolic way of Absalom's descent into crime?

HISTORICAL BACKGROUND

The South African problems Paton wrote about in 1946 were still present in the mid-1980s. In 1984, the black Anglican Bishop Desmond Tutu was awarded the prestigious Nobel Peace Prize for his efforts toward a nonviolent solution of South Africa's racial problems. The basic social problems that concerned Bishop Tutu as well as Paton can be summed up in one word—*apartheid*. Apartheid-Afrikaans for "apartness" or "segregation"—means, in theory, that different races should develop separately along their own paths. In practice, it means white supremacy in an overwhelmingly nonwhite nation. When Paton wrote *Cry, the Beloved Country* apartheid was not yet official government policy as it became in 1948 but much of the apartheid system was already part of the law. Some understanding of the historical background of South Africa and apartheid will help you better understand the events in *Cry, the Beloved Country*.

The area now known as South Africa was colonized by the Dutch East India Company near the Cape of Good Hope in the second half of the 17th century. The early settlers brought smallpox, which killed many San (Bushmen) and Khoikhoi (Hottentots) of the area. To provide labor, the Company imported large numbers of slaves from West Africa and Malaya. At first, the Company encouraged racially mixed marriages, but as large numbers of Dutch, German, and French Huguenot immigrants joined the Colony, the practice was forbidden. This mixture of cultures produced an offshoot of the Dutch language that came to be known as Afrikaans. The European settlers were known as "Boers," the Dutch word for farmer.

Racial groupings were fairly well established by 1814, the year Britain acquired Cape Colony as a result of the Napoleonic Wars in Europe. The first English settlers, mostly government employees, antagonized the Afrikaans-speaking Boers. The Boers resented what they saw as government meddling and injustice; for instance, the abolition of slavery with little or no financial compensation and the restriction on acquiring new land. As early as 1702 some Boers had begun to trek (journey) inland, and the British presence led to increased movement inland by Boers.

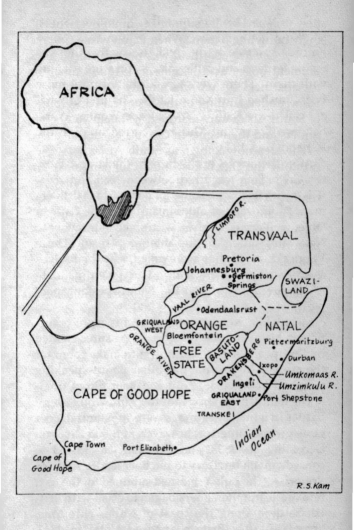

Union of South Africa in 1946

The early Trekkers met the Xhosa, a Bantu-speaking black ethnic group, whom they called Kaffirs. As a rule, early Trekkers saw the Xhosa as fellow farmers and cattle-raisers and were friendly with them. There were few hostilities until more Boers pushed into Xhosa lands. The first of what are called the Kaffir Wars or Cape Frontier Wars, between Boers and Xhosa, occurred in 1779; the last ended in 1879.

After the arrival of the British, the largest Trek, the Great Trek, occurred between 1835 and 1843. It is estimated that some 12,000 to 14,000 Boers moved hundreds of miles inland from the Cape in large, well-armed parties, with some journeying to Natal and others to the interior plateau. These Voortrekkers, as they were called, saw themselves as Christian pioneers with a God-given mandate to subdue the land and the Bantu-speaking peoples.

Meanwhile roughly similar events were occurring in Natal and the Transvaal. Pressures created by Europeans led the Zulu first to make room for themselves by driving out other Bantu-speaking peoples. About 1836, Zulu and Boer forces finally clashed. Under Dingaan, the Zulu won several battles in which Boer losses were substantial. Boer guns proved superior, however, at Blood River on December 16, 1838, and Dingaan was forced to concede much territory to the Boer leader Andries Pretorius. The Zulu remained subdued for the next few years, but then Boers began to clash with British settlers along the coast of Natal. This time, especially after Britain annexed Natal in 1843, many Boers simply moved inland.

Recognizing the political reality, Britain granted

independent status to the Boers of the Transvaal
Republic in 1852 and to the Orange Free State in
1854. In 1879 British domination of Natal became
complete, with the crushing of a last Zulu army.
By that time the Xhosa in Cape Province had also
been overwhelmed by surrounding Europeans.

From about 1870 on, discoveries of diamonds
and gold brought a new influx of whites into the
Orange Free State and the Transvaal. The miners
who established Johannesburg in 1886 included
more men speaking English than Afrikaans. These
"uitlanders" (outlanders or foreigners), as the Boer
government called them, were taxed heavily but
not allowed to vote. Not surprisingly, the outlanders supported British attempts to annex Griqua-
land West in 1871 and the Transvaal in 1877, and
tension mounted. The simmering conflict led to
the South African, or Boer, War of 1899–1902. At
first the British lost to Boer raids, but they won
after they began to burn conquered lands and to
put more than 100,000 Afrikaner women and children in detention camps. The camps were so
crowded and unsanitary that as many as 26,000
people died of typhoid fever.

In 1910 the British united Cape Colony, Transvaal, the Orange Free State, and Natal into the
Union of South Africa. As a country with domin-
ion status, South Africa recognized the British
monarch as head of state, but largely governed
itself. Whites controlled the new country.

Afrikaners took politics seriously, and soon rose
to prominence in the government of South Africa.
Some Boer leaders tried to mend rifts between
English-speaking and Afrikaans-speaking whites.
Two whose names appear in *Cry, the Beloved Coun-*

try are Botha and Smuts. Louis Botha (1862–1919), the first Prime Minister, allied South Africa with the British in World War I. The Prime Minister in the early 1920s was the leader of the Unionist party, Jan Christiaan Smuts (1870–1950).

Many Afrikaners, however, and some South Africans of English ancestry as well, resented the relatively moderate policies of Botha and Smuts. They united in the Nationalist party founded by James Barry Hertzog, Prime Minister from 1924 to 1939. Hertzog led an Afrikaner cultural revival, pushed for cutting back the voting rights of nonwhites, and promoted the establishment of reserved lands for black Africans as their permanent homes. (Reserves were not new. Some had been established in Natal as early as the 1870s.) The last five years Hertzog was Prime Minister, his party joined that of Smuts in the United South African National party. But this alliance disintegrated at the outbreak of World War II in 1939. In that year, Smuts again became Prime Minister, and he led South Africa into World War II on the Allied side. He also brought South Africa into the United Nations in 1945 as a charter member.

With the election victory of the Nationalist party of Daniel F. Malan (1874–1959) in 1948, the practice of apartheid became official policy. It called for the elimination of existing integration, as in schools, labor unions, and places like opera houses, and greatly curtailed the political, economic, educational, and social opportunities of nonwhites. The ultimate goal became the division of the country into separate areas for whites and nonwhites. By the mid-1980s, several "independent homelands" for black ethnic groups had been established.

The great majority of nonwhites were opposed to apartheid, but the need to earn a living forced them to take part in the system. There was racial conflict, however, and it continued into the 1980s. Nonviolent protest movements of nonwhites were met in some instances with violence by the government—notably at Sharpville in 1960 and at Soweto in 1976. In some cases nonwhites used violence to press for change. The white-minority government made scattered concessions to nonwhites, but the basic dispute over the proper path of development remained. Whites generally sought to maintain their privileged position of controlling the country's political and economic life, while many nonwhites aimed to establish a democratic society in which persons would have equal opportunities regardless of race.

Some changes occurred in South Africa in the 40 years following publication of *Cry, the Beloved Country.* But basic issues discussed in the novel— the causes, effects, and possible end of racial segregation—remained very relevant to life in the country in the 1980s.

THEMES

In a speech quoted in the Introduction to *Cry, the Beloved Country*, Alan Paton tells us that the central theme of his novel is the deterioration of black men's character in the slums of white men's cities. Deterioration of the traditional culture is indeed central to the story, but Paton presents more than that. Most readers see two main themes in *Cry, the Beloved Country*—first, the theme of decay Paton describes, and, second, a theme of rebuilding through compassion or love. Other themes, such as the deadliness of fear, the horrible consequences of discrimination, the relationship between the land and the people, the role of chance or accident in life, and the place of spiritual values, are woven into these two main themes.

The Breakdown of the Tribe

Book I of the novel deals most strongly with tribal breakdown, and Book II centers on crime among black youths, with Absalom Kumalo as a sample case. Almost immediately in Book I we note Stephen Kumalo's worried thoughts, but don't understand what he means by the "breakdown of the tribe" until he arrives in Johannesburg. As the story progresses, you learn that the members of his own family no longer see each other, that his sister found it necessary to support herself by crime, that his brother has abandoned religious values and moral standards based on family unity, that his son is a thief, and that his brother and nephew will lie to save themselves no matter what effect this has on other members of the family.

For the most part, you become aware of the pressures on blacks only gradually. Your awareness grows as Kumalo's does, during his search for his son. Sometimes a specific chapter is crammed with examples—for example, Chapter 9 on housing, Chapter 12 on crime, and Chapter 23 on the gold strike at Odendaalsrust. Outside the cities, causes of moral decay and tribal breakdown include the assignment of blacks to lands too poor for good farming, and the siphoning off of workers to mines where the pay is poor and working conditions are dangerous. In the cities, breakdown is caused by lack of jobs and laws of separation that do not provide blacks with housing and other facilities equivalent to those available to whites.

Wound through everything is fear. Whites fear not just black crime, but also a black uprising if speakers such as John Kumalo are allowed too much leeway. Blacks fear white retaliation for strikes and boycotts. Kumalo is afraid to know what has happened to his son; his son is afraid of what his father will say; the girl is afraid of life in general; John is afraid of the police. Fear is almost a climate of life, and whites are depicted as the ones to blame.

Rebuilding in Compassion

Already in Book I the theme of the power of love or compassion is shown in Msimangu's speech to Kumalo after they have left John Kumalo's shop in Chapter 7. It is shown, too, in the lives of such blacks as Msimangu and Kumalo themselves, and the black leader Dubula. All values have not deteriorated after all, or these three would not be men of principle. Hope for the future is also shown by white men who defy the customs and laws of apartheid to give rides to blacks who are boycotting buses. Then there are the young white man from the reformatory and Mr. Carmichael. The reformatory official genuinely cares about the young blacks in his care, and Mr. Carmichael takes Absalom's case for free.

In Book II the theme appears primarily in the writings of Arthur Jarvis (Chapters 20 and 21) and in the reconciliation between Stephen Kumalo and James Jarvis. It also appears in Absalom's repentance and in his girl's growing desire to change, to start a new life. In Book III the theme blossoms.

Jarvis comes to see Kumalo no longer as pitiful, timid, stupid, and maybe not even very clean, but as a good man, a pastor beloved of his people, a man with a vision for the future. Kumalo in turn comes to see Jarvis no longer as practically a god, but as a caring father, husband, and employer who has grown willing to spend his money to help the people of Ndotsheni make better use of their land. One black man and one white man, at least, begin to work together on the only terms Msimangu and Arthur Jarvis considered workable—a willingness to work with others, whatever their race, out of a shared love of one's country.

Moreover there are the children—Gertrude's son, the grandchild to be born, and especially the small white boy, Arthur's son, who has already begun to follow in his father's footsteps. In them Paton suggests a readiness for change, a willingness to create a new kind of life for all South Africans.

STYLE

In some ways Paton is a very realistic writer. He is dealing with things he has experienced in his own life, and he is able to describe people, cities, landscapes, and events in a factual way.

Paton occasionally uses symbols. Some of the names that may be symbolic are discussed in a note within Chapter 2 in The Story section of this guidebook. Sometimes a meal is presented almost as a communion service, and the titihoya bird seems to be a symbol for the land itself. The titihoya has deserted the barren land around Ndotsheni, but still cries on the rich farms up-

land. Its cry is an appeal to the people to love
and care for the land. Some readers see symbolic
value in mountains and uplands as good places,
and valleys as places of moral decay, but others
feel it's stretching a point to accept that interpretation. (Consider the fact that Johannesburg is at
a higher elevation than Ixopo.)

What is remarkable about Paton's style is the
fresh sound of his language. On the first page you
will probably notice that the main style does not
follow patterns of written and spoken English to
which you are accustomed. In contrast, the more
common patterns of English, used principally in
the novel when a white man is thinking or speaking, (1) sound harsh and to the point, (2) involve
a vocabulary that includes slang, and (3) are more
complicated than Paton's main style.

The special style Paton invented for this book
involves very simple vocabulary, and makes use
of biblical patterns as well as those of Zulu and
other Bantu languages. This style incudes (1) symbols so natural that we hardly think of them as
symbols, such as light and darkness; (2) short
clauses connected by *but* or *and*; and (3) repetition.
Parallel statements often say the same thing twice
in slightly different words. This primary style is
used to represent speech or thoughts "translated"
from Zulu and to give comments from the omniscient narrator.

Both styles can be seen in Chapter 22 where the
prosecutor's style of speech contrasts with Absalom's. After a while, though, even the prosecutor
begins to fall into Absalom's simpler speech patterns. The more common English style shows up

best in conversations of white men. For example, Harrison says this to Jarvis: "They get good balanced food, far better than they'd ever get at home, free medical attention, and God knows what. I tell you, Jarvis, if mining costs go up much more there won't be any mines." You may or may not agree with Harrison, but the points are so clearly presented that you don't have to think to know what is meant.

The main style, the Zulu-biblical one, appears in lines like these: "The great valley of the Umzimkulu is still in darkness, but the light will come there. Ndotsheni is still in darkness, but the light will come there also." Other good examples occur in the scene between Kumalo and Jarvis at the Smith house, when both are speaking Zulu. For instance, Jarvis says, "I have heard you. I understand what I did not understand. There is no anger in me." This style demands more of the reader. It's up to you to recall all earlier evidence and deduce just what it is that Jarvis understands.

You will probably respond to Paton's heavy use of his understated Zulu-biblical style with considerable emotion. To get a better feel for Paton's language, it might help to formulate an observation in two ways. For example, Paton could have written a sentence like this, in ordinary English: "The rounded green hills are too pretty for words." Instead he wrote this: "These hills are grass-covered and rolling, and they are lovely beyond any singing of it." Most of you will feel a kind of inner ache at the beauty of that sentence. The style lifts descriptions and events above the ordinary, and may lead you to feel a kind of reverence usually reserved for the Bible itself.

POINT OF VIEW

Novels are written in either the first or the third person point of view. In first-person point of view, someone in the story is narrating it. In third-person narration, an unnamed person outside the story is telling it. Two kinds of third-person narration are used in *Cry, the Beloved Country*. One type of third-person narration is by an omniscient or all-knowing viewer who sees everything. The opening and closing paragraphs of most chapters are of this type and so are the chapters composed of a dozen or more bits and pieces of the dialog of many different people.

In other parts of the novel the point of view is what is called third-person limited—the narrator has you focus on events through the eyes and ears and mind of one specific character. That character is usually Stephen Kumalo, but there are places in the novel where the focus shifts, and you find yourself looking through the eyes of Mrs. Lithebe or James Jarvis. Each time the focus shifts, you will probably feel it. It's slightly jarring, and can be confusing until you figure out whose mind you've entered. Watch for lines of asterisks in the text and the beginnings of chapters. These are visual cues that the point of view may be shifting.

Paton accomplishes two things by using a combination of third-person omniscient and third-person limited point of view. First, he lets you get to know, care about, and appreciate Stephen Kumalo as a person. Second, he presents an overview of what many people in South Africa are thinking and saying, whether they are black or white, Afrikaans or English.

FORM AND STRUCTURE

Cry, the Beloved Country is what is called a problem or sociological novel. The social issue is racial discrimination in South Africa. Some critics even call *Cry, the Beloved Country* a propaganda novel, because it shows the evils of discrimination so strongly.

Another novel of this type is John Steinbeck's *The Grapes of Wrath* (1939), which deals with the problems of migrant workers. Paton had been reading and thinking about *The Grapes of Wrath* just before he began writing *Cry, the Beloved Country*, and that may account for one way the books are alike in structure. Both use what are called intercalary or inserted chapters. These are chapters like 9, 12, and 23 in *Cry, the Beloved Country*, chapters that give you a picture of what is happening in society as a whole. They do not directly advance the plot, but skipping them would rob you of a full understanding of the setting of the story.

Another thing to notice about the structure of *Cry, the Beloved Country* is that it is circular. The novel begins in a rural area of Natal, moves to Johannesburg, and returns again to Ndotsheni in Natal.

Paton presents the plot and themes of his novel in a three-part structure. Book I (Chapters 1 to 17) starts off the basic plot as a search. Stephen Kumalo attempts to locate and reunite the members of his family, especially his son. The high points come when Arthur Jarvis is killed and Absalom Kumalo is arrested. The theme of tribal disintegration is stronger than the other main theme of rebuilding in Book I.

The intensity continues to build in Book II (Chapters 18 to 29). The trial progresses, intercalary chapters provide a fuller picture of social issues, and you see what happens when the two fathers meet. Some of the intercalary chapters contain as many as a dozen separate scenes, and many of them use so much dramatic dialog that they could easily be presented as brief plays. Both major themes occur in Book II, but the breakdown of the traditional order still seems to outweigh the theme of rebuilding.

Book III (Chapters 30 to 36) is the resolution, or working out, of the plot. Kumalo and Jarvis begin to cooperate to change the village of Ndotsheni. Here the stress is on rebuilding, a promise of hope for the future.

The Story

AUTHOR'S NOTES AND INTRODUCTION

Cry, the Beloved Country begins with two Author's Notes and an Introduction. Part of the original Author's Note (written when *Cry, the Beloved Country* was first published) presents an analysis of the 1948 population of South Africa. Paton lists the major groups as Afrikaans-speaking whites, English-speaking whites, Indians, Coloureds (people of mixed ancestry), and blacks. Percentage computations based on Paton's figures show that in 1948 blacks formed approximately 59 percent of a total population of about 11 million. Whites accounted for about 30 percent of the population, with those speaking English making up less than one fourth of the whites (about 7 percent of the total population). All other groups accounted for about 11 percent of the population.

The figures are relevant because the story concentrates on one black family and one English-speaking white family. In the story, Paton doesn't keep reminding you that white English-speakers are a small minority, and that the white family may therefore not be typical of *all* whites. Nor does he keep saying that the problem of the black family may be multiplied in many families, since blacks form so large a part of the population. He expects you to combine population data from this note with clues in the story, and to reach your own conclusions about racial problems in South African society.

The Second Author's Note updates the population information for a later edition of the novel. It reports a total 1959 population of about 15 million, with Indian, Coloured, and black people a larger proportion of the total than in 1948.

NOTE: In 1980 the government reported that the population of South Africa was about 25 million. Some two thirds of these people were said to be black, approximately 18 percent were white, about 10 percent were Coloured (persons of mixed ancestry), and roughly 4 percent were Asian.

The bulk of the Introduction consists of several pages quoted from a speech by Alan Paton. These pages convey Paton's deep feelings for his country, and the historical facts they outline are generally accurate. However, we use some terms differently now. For instance, San and Khoikhoi are used instead of Bushmen and Hottentots; Xosa is more often spelled Xhosa; and the Anglo-Boer War is usually called the South African War.

Paton's comment that Afrikaans-speaking people are descendants of the Dutch is only partly accurate. The Dutch East India Company founded Cape Colony, but the Dutch did not settle in large numbers. Recent studies give the ethnic origins of Afrikaners as 45% German, 27% French, 22% Dutch, and 6% "other."

Paton conveys very well how he thinks Afikaners came to perceive blacks as dangerous and to fear them enough to want to establish a system of racial segregation. Some Afrikaners, however, would add religious belief as a basis for segregation. Some Afrikaners interpret passages of the Bible on the descendants of Noah's sons to mean that God wants total separation of the races, and that whites are naturally superior. Paton explains that some whites struggle with their own consciences over racial segregation. You'll find a fuller expression of this struggle later in the novel in a paper written by Arthur Jarvis.

BOOK I (CHAPTERS 1–17): THE SEARCH

CHAPTER 1

In Chapter 1 the narrator stands on a hill, looking around at valleys and mountains, a river and hills. Some names, like the Zulu *Umzimkulu* (a river and valley in Natal), and some words, like the Afrikaans *kloof* (a ravine), establish the South African setting. The Drakensberg (which means "dragon mountains") is a large mountain range dividing the Orange Free State from Natal. The narrator says that in the hills of Natal the soil is so rich it seems "holy, being even as it came from the Creator." Nothing has been done to harm it. But in the valley below, the land is red and bare. Sharp stones and grass hurt the feet. Food is so scarce that even the titihoya bird has left. The maize (corn) does not grow tall, and the red earth is so eroded that when it rains the muddy land seems to flow with blood. The land is ruined, and so are families. Men and young people have gone somewhere else, and only old people, women, and children stay. What has caused the damage to the land and desertion by the young? You'll see in coming chapters.

NOTE: Point of View and Style   At this point you can't tell who is speaking to you—a situation that means the book is written from a point of view called third person omniscient. That is, some all-knowing viewer outside the story, someone you won't really be conscious of as the story continues, is telling it. This narrator is not the author himself, but a story-teller created by the author.

The language of the narrator is beautiful. You'll immediately notice its difference from ordinary English. Its patterns are meant to echo African languages and parts of the Bible. This style will be used not only by the all-knowing story-teller, but also by the man we meet in Chapter 2—a man whose first language is Zulu, one of the Bantu family of languages, and whose second language, English, he encounters mostly in the Bible.

CHAPTER 2

In Chapter 2 you meet Reverend Stephen Kumalo. A little girl makes it clear that he is respected. She hesitates to enter "so important a house" as his, courteously addresses him not by name but as "umfundisi" (Reverend), and only then says she has brought something from the white man at the store. The name Kumalo, the word umfundisi, and the mention that the sender is white indicate that Kumalo must be black. His language also suggests a nonwhite culture, when he kindly sends the little girl to "the mother," his wife, for something to eat.

Only then does he look at what the child has given him. It's a letter, shabby from passing through many hands. Before opening it, he thinks about his brother John, a carpenter, who has a business now in Johannesburg. His sister Gertrude, 25 years younger than he, is in Johannesburg, too. She took her little boy and went to look for her missing husband. His only son, Absalom, went there also. None have returned, and neither have other relatives. It's as if the city had swallowed them up.

NOTE: Absalom and Other Names Absalom is such an unusual name that you can be sure you're meant to think of the Absalom of the Bible. A favorite son of King David, he was a handsome young man proud of his long, luxuriant hair. The story, told in 2 Samuel, depicts Absalom as restless and wicked. David ignored Absalom's insults until he joined David's enemies in armed rebellion. Ironically, his spectacular hair caused Absalom's downfall. He rode beneath a tree, and his flowing hair caught in a branch. David's men were able to kill him as he hung there. Instead of rejoicing, David bitterly mourned Absalom's death. Absalom Kumalo has already caused his father grief by disappearing to Johannesburg, and the Bible story is so famous that the very name Absalom suggests trouble to come—perhaps even the boy's death.

Other characters in the novel have names from the Gospels and the Acts of the Apostles, but they don't leap out at you because the names are more common than Absalom. One, for example, is Stephen. The Stephen in the Bible was a deacon of the early church. His job was to handle members' complaints. A courageous man, he became the first Christian martyr when he was stoned to death for his beliefs. There are two Johns in the Gospels. One is John the Baptist, the cousin of Jesus, a preacher who attracted huge crowds. The other John was an apostle, the hot-tempered son of Zebedee and brother of James, an equally hot-tempered man. Both brothers, originally fishermen, became leaders in the early church. John was also known as an apostle especially close to and loved by Jesus. Another name that will come up in *Cry, the Beloved Country* is Matthew, a tax collector at the time of Jesus. People hated tax collectors for routinely extorting additional money for their own use, but Jesus made Matthew an apostle anyway.

You will also find the name Arthur in the novel. Arthur is not a biblical name, but to English-speaking people it suggests King Arthur, the Knights of the Round Table, and Camelot. Arthur, like Jesus Christ, had both a mission in life and devoted disciples.

Kumalo is reluctant to open the letter. He obviously doesn't receive many. His reaction is the kind people had years ago when the telephone operator would say, "long distance calling." In the early days of telephones, long distance calls usually meant bad news. Naturally enough, therefore, people panicked at receiving a long distance call. Kumalo has that kind of reaction to the letter. He examines it from every angle and even asks his wife if she'd been expecting one. Then she starts guessing, too. They both seem to hope it has to do with Absalom. Mrs. Kumalo finally opens it, "reading as a Zulu who reads English."

NOTE: English as a Second Language "Zulu" completes the identification of the Kumalos as blacks. The Zulu are a large ethnic group whose language belongs to the Bantu family of languages. Many Bantu-speakers in South Africa also speak Afrikaans or English. The Kumalos obviously read English, but seem awkward with it, as one often is with a second language.

The letter is from the Reverend Theophilus Msimangu. It's short and to the point. Msimangu wants Kumalo to come to Sophiatown in Johannesburg at once, because Kumalo's sister, Gertrude, is sick.

The Kumalos are silent for awhile, and you can imagine why. The reports from Johannesburg make the city seem dangerous. Still, what can they do? This concerns family. They have a cocoa tin containing money set aside for Absalom's education at a school called St. Chad's. Kumalo says he can't use it, but his wife asks why not? Absalom won't be using it. Why does that make Kumalo angry? If you've ever deliberately chosen not to face something, you understand why. He could kid himself that his son would come back as long as he never admitted aloud that the boy was gone for good. The truth hurts, so he shouts at his wife as if it were her fault that nobody writes.

But Kumalo quickly calms down. He agrees to use the money. It's not all that much—at 1946 exchange rates, 12 pounds, 5 shillings, and 7 pence came to about $50 in U.S. currency. He thinks he can manage on two thirds of it, but his wife is more realistic. She urges him to take it all, and also another 10 pounds (about $40) they've been saving. Her sense of duty must be strong: they need the money for a stove or clothes. But the decision is made, and Kumalo will notify the Bishop about his absence from St. Mark's. He goes off to pray, and she lays her head on the table. What does that simple action manage somehow to suggest to you?

A line of asterisks on the page marks the passage of time. The narrator quotes what sounds like a saying, "All roads lead to Johannesburg." It echoes "All roads lead to Rome," and suggests how important a city Johannesburg must be for South Africans. The narrator says trains head there all night long on tracks cut through hills and valleys, while the country sleeps, and adds, "Happy the eyes that can close." This could simply mean the ride is rough, but it's more likely a different way of stating the idea that people without worries are lucky.

NOTE: Johannesburg   Johannesburg is a major hub of South Africa's transportation network, as the last paragraph of Chapter 2 suggests. It isn't the country's capital, but it is the largest city and a leading manufacturing and banking center. The richest gold strikes in South African history occurred in the Johannesburg area, and gold miners established the city near their claims in 1886. Today Johannesburg is still the center of the important South African gold-mining industry.

CHAPTER 3

Kumalo's journey begins with a walk from Ndotsheni to the train station in nearby Carisbrooke, at the edge of the Drakensberg Mountains. He is so cautious that he arrives an hour early, though the local train is so small and slow that nearly anyone could catch up, even if it had left already. The valley below is sometimes made mysterious by mist, and sometimes filled with beauty. People waiting can hear the train whistle at each stop below.

But Kumalo doesn't notice these things. He's busy worrying whether his money will last, how sick his sister is, and whether you can really go up and down the streets of Johannesburg forever without backtracking. He recalls a village boy who stepped off a Johannesburg curb and was killed by a truck. But he worries most of all about what has become of Absalom.

Finally the train nears. At the last minute the man who helped Kumalo with his bag asks a favor for another man, Sibeko. Sibeko was embarrassed to ask directly, since he is not a member of the church. Kumalo recognizes him as a fellow black and agrees to look for Sibeko's daughter. The problem is like his own. Sibeko hasn't heard from the girl since she followed her white mistress, Smith's daughter, to the Johannesburg suburb of Springs.

The coach Kumalo boards is warm and smelly. It's for nonwhites; whites have their own coaches. The black men on this coach wear European clothing, but some of the women combine European with traditional Zulu dress or wrap themselves in blankets. The people notice Kumalo's priestly collar and make room for him. He automatically looks around for someone of his own standing, an action that shows us he is aware of the respect other blacks hold for him. In fact, when he turns to the window to say goodbye to his friend, he shows a little vanity as well. He loudly repeats his promise to look for the girl, although he has much to do in the city. "It is always so," he says, as if he went there often. Then the train jerks and he nearly falls. He quickly regains his dignity and sits, enjoying his harmless vanity. But the good feeling soon fades, and he becomes again simply a scared black country priest heading into an alien world that he believes has damaged his own world beyond repair.

CHAPTER 4

This chapter is a delightful version of a classic plot—country boy goes to the big, bad city. The length of the trip, both physically and emotionally, is conveyed partly by the catalog of names. From Carisbrooke it's seven miles to Ixopo, and then it's up and down through hills, valleys, and towns with Zulu, English, and Afrikaans names—Lufafa and Umkomaas, Eastwolds and Donnybrook, Elandskop and Pietermaritzburg. At Pietermaritzburg, Kumalo changes to a cable-drawn train mechanically hoisted up the Drakensberg mountains. He sleeps, waking again at dawn to find his train connected to a regular engine and moving across the veld, a vast highland plain leading toward Johannesburg.

NOTE: Pietermaritzburg   Pietermaritzburg is the capital of the province of Natal. The city was founded in 1839 by Boers of the Great Trek led by Piet Retief and Gerrit Maritz. Iron ore is mined nearby and the city is an industrial center. It also has a university campus. Tourists often visit the Church of the Vow, built to commemorate the 1838 Boer victory over Zulu forces led by Dingaan.

Since Kumalo's earlier companions are no longer on board, he drops his sophisticated pose and eagerly asks questions. He learns how the white men use dynamite (fire-sticks) to blast out the gold mines, and how the black men send up the rubble in a cage powered by a great iron wheel. The spokes

move so fast they trick the eye (the phenomenon
where a speeding wheel appears to turn slowly in
reverse). The mining camp looks so vast that he
asks if it's Johannesburg. The others laugh. Johannesburg is incomparably larger. Later, passing many
buildings and "streets without number," Kumalo
asks again whether this is Johannesburg. Again
they laugh. "This is nothing." Kumalo, however,
is overwhelmed by trains roaring past his own,
and the sight of more stations, people, and streets
than he has ever imagined.

Still traveling at dusk, Kumalo sees great buildings lit up in a way new to him. One set of lights
shows a bottle endlessly pouring water, but he can't
understand why the words read "black and white"
when the lights are red and green. You'll probably
smile, recognizing a neon liquor ad. Does the brand
name stike you as ironic? Why do you think Paton
included this detail?

Finally the train stops in a great underground
station—Johannesburg at last. Although he is buf-
feted by the crowds and overwhelmed by the noise,
Kumalo successfully navigates to street level, only
to be baffled anew by traffic. He tries to cross a
street on green as he was told, but a bus swings
into his path. He scurries back in terror, shrinking
against a wall and praying to God for protection.

A young black man who speaks understandable
Zulu seems to be the answer to his prayer, but
Kumalo is smart enough not to give his trust immediately. Instead, his suitcase growing heavier
by the second, he follows, lost in wonder as the
young man boldly crosses street after street and
makes entlless twists and turns to reach the proper
bus stop. By then Kumalo is so impressed, he will-

ingly hands over a pound (about $4) so the young man can buy him a bus ticket. But the street-wise youth does not return, because there is no ticket office. Kumalo has been cheated.

All he can do is to approach a kindly looking older man. This man abandons his own errand and not only escorts Kumalo onto the correct bus, but right to the door of the Mission House in Sophiatown. On the way, Kumalo is awed by the swaying ride. He gawks out the windows and marvels at the casual skill of the driver and the tremendous courage it must take to drive through such confusion. By the time they reach the Mission House, Kumalo has lost all vanity. Humbly, he tells Msimangu how much he owes his guide. Msimangu introduces the guide as Mr. Mafolo, "one of our big business men, and a good son of the Church." Safe at last, Kumalo, who doesn't usually smoke, accepts a cigarette and sinks into a big chair. The Mission House is to him a place of safety, securely shutting out the bewildering wonders of Johannesburg.

NOTE: Religion and Language in South Africa
Several clues suggested that Kumalo's religion was Anglican even before Mr. Mafolo says, "I too am an Anglican." The Anglican Church, or Church of England, has bishops and married priests, and English is used in services. St. Mark's and St. Chad's are also typical Anglican names for institutions. There are some differences between the training of black and white Anglican priests, however. Kumalo has obviously never been to Johannesburg before, and must therefore have been educated in

schools in Natal. Later in the novel, a white priest translates a Latin phrase for Kumalo, suggesting that white priests receive a broader education. In 1946 black and white congregations of the same religion were sometimes allowed to use the same church buildings for services at different times, but even this practice was outlawed after 1948 when apartheid became public policy. Black and white people do attend the same funeral later in the novel, but it is clearly considered unusual. It's little wonder, then, that Kumalo is surprised in Chapter 5 to find black and white priests mixing at the Mission House.

Whether black or white, Anglicans do not constitute the largest Christian church in South Africa. In 1980 there were about 1.3 million Anglicans compared with 12 million Methodists, 5 million members of independent black churches, and 2.8 million members of the Dutch Reformed Church, among other denominations. The independent black churches combine elements of Christianity and traditional African belief systems.

As for different languages among blacks, it's not surprising that the young black who fooled Kumalo was not Zulu. Although the government has used the word *Bantu* to mean all blacks in the Republic of South Africa, the word is usually used to refer to a family of African languages. In east, central, and southern Africa there are hundreds of Bantu languages spoken by more than 80 million blacks—Swahili is a well-known Bantu language. In South Africa the largest language groups include Zulu, Xhosa, Sotho, and Tswana. Many blacks speak Afrikaans or English as well. Among whites, about 60 percent speak Afrikaans as their first language, and some 40 percent speak English. Most Coloureds speak Afrikaans.

CHAPTER 5

New marvels await Kumalo, however, even inside the Mission House—indoor plumbing, hot, cold, and flushable; multiple plates and silverware at the table; black and white priests eating *together*. The priests beg for news of the rural areas. Kumalo reports, stressing how the traditional tribal structure is breaking down. They in turn tell Kumalo the breakdown is worse in the city. All of white Johannesburg fears young black men, and they do too since the night some young blacks attacked a black girl in Sophiatown. One begins to wonder— how does Absalom make his living?

After dinner, Kumalo meets privately with Msimangu. Msimangu tells Kumalo that Gertrude's sickness, grave as it is, is not physical. Instead of *no* husband, he says, "It would be truer to say . . . that she has many husbands."

NOTE: This is a sort of priest-to-priest shorthand. It paraphrases what Jesus said to a Samaritan woman who claimed she had no husband: "You are right. . . , for, although you have had five husbands, the man with whom you are now living is not your husband." It means that Gertrude is a prostitute.

Kumalo's immediate understanding is shown by

his cry of "Tixo! Tixo!" (God! God!) But the story gets worse. Gertrude lives in Claremont, the "garbage heap" of Johannesburg. She makes and sells bad liquor and sleeps with anyone who can pay her price. Gambling, drinking, stabbings, even a murder have occurred at her place. And she has been in prison. Shaken, Kumalo refuses a calming cigarette, and absorbs this new information.

Then, with some embarrassment, he asks about Absalom and his brother John. Msimangu knows nothing of Absalom, but says that John has no use for the church anymore. John argues, "what God has not done for South Africa, man must do." Kumalo does not want the church to look bad, and wonders what the Bishop will think of a priest with such relatives. Msimangu says the Bishop knows that tragedies can occur even in a priest's family. Kumalo already knows about the whites' assigning blacks poor lands, and almost accidentally enticing the young to leave their families and come to the cities. Without repeating that information, Msimangu says it is white men's fault that young blacks abandon strict tribal morals and slide into crime. It doesn't seem possible to go back to old tribal ways, and neither blacks nor whites seem to know what should replace the old patterns. Msimangu is perplexed. If God has allowed white men to cause all this destruction, why does he send so few whites who even try to find ways to rebuild what their own kind have broken down?

Msimangu leaves Kumalo for the night, at a room in the house of Mrs. Lithebe, an old Msutu woman who speaks Zulu. Temporarily released from other duties, Msimangu will be back in the morning to give his time to Kumalo. Alone for the first time since he left home, Kumalo just stands there.

Physical, mental, and emotional overload make it hard for him to believe that only two days have passed since he first held Msimangu's letter. At this point in the novel, do you have the feeling that things will work out well for Kumalo and his family? What is your evidence?

CHAPTER 6

In the morning Kumalo sets out to confront Gertrude. On the way, he learns about racial separation in Johannesburg, including separate buses for whites and blacks. The police can't keep up with disturbances created by white roughnecks and black youths, too, Msimangu says. When they pass the building of *The Bantu Press*, the black newspaper, Msimangu comments that John and his friends call it *The Bantu Repress*. Kumalo doesn't pick up on the remark. As yet he does not directly associate his own problems with repression in the cities.

But the Claremont district shocks him—children not in school, houses shabby, streets filthy despite beautiful names. Msimangu leaves Kumalo at Gertrude's door on Hyacinth Street. When she answers his knock, fear fills her eyes. Why, you may wonder? What does she think her brother will do? She doesn't let him in until her gamblers clear out, and by then she has gained composure. Her voice is hard, but her thin defenses crumble at Kumalo's anger. She falls to the floor crying, protesting that she wants to leave, but is too bad to go back home. Kumalo softens quickly, as he did when angry with his wife in Ndotsheni. His normal kindliness returns, and he and Gertrude pray together—quietly though, lest the neighbors laugh.

Gertrude agrees to pack up her belongings and

her child—a small boy who has come into the room with a runny nose and dirty clothes—and move to Mrs. Lithebe's. When Kumalo asks about Absalom, though, she can't tell him much—just that he used to spend his time with his cousin, John Kumalo's son.

With Msimangu's help, Gertrude moves the same day. Mrs. Lithebe welcomes the woman and boy, and Kumalo is ecstatic. He's only been in the city a day, and already the tribe is being rebuilt, and a soul has been restored. Most readers feel a little skeptical, though. Can Gertrude's change of heart be trusted? Will she really be able to go back to village life?

CHAPTER 7

The next day, Kumalo starts searching for Absalom. He has already written his wife about the news so far, and has bought some decent clothes for Gertrude and the boy. Can you see that Kumalo's actions are both practical and symbolic? It's not just that Gertrude's clothes are too filthy to save. Clothes symbolize a style of living, too. Have you ever bought a new outfit, or carefully planned an ensemble, so that you would fit into a group on a special occasion? You can see, then, that the new clothes are closely linked Gertrude's new life as a respectable young mother. (If she should happen to go back to prostitution, what do you predict might happen to the new clothes?)

Selling Gertrude's possessions is equally symbolic. It's like cleaning out files or closets for a fresh start. As for money, Kumalo finds it strange that his sister saved nothing when she earned so much.

But we can understand: she's a gambler, something Kumalo wouldn't be able to grasp. After all, he and his wife had managed to save money even on his small salary of 8 pounds per month.

NOTE: Exchange rate   Today, South Africa's currency is called the rand, but in 1946 the old British system of pounds, shillings, and pence was used. At that time a South African pound was equivalent to $4.03, a shilling to 20 cents, and a penny to 1.6 cents.

Later, walking to John's shop with Msimangu, Kumalo decides it's true that the streets in Johannesburg seem endless. As for John, he has grown fat and has changed greatly. It's already been ten years since his wife Esther left him for being unfaithful, and he hasn't married the woman he lives with now. But he has a telephone and he earns 8 to 12 pounds a *week*. John prefers to speak English (what does that suggest to you?), and his oratory moves even his brother. He speaks of laws that favor the whites, mines that produce fortunes for whites while blacks toil there for three shillings a day, bishops in fine houses who criticize the laws but do not act, and white priests who earn six times what his brother gets. But John has been unable to persuade his own son to stay with him, and all he knows of Absalom is that he used to work at the Doornfontein Textiles Company in Sophiatown.

Back on the street, the priests discuss John. He is an influential speaker who could lead blacks to

riot if he chose. Later you learn that black leaders
do not respect John, but do value his effective
speaking voice. Msimangu admits that much of
what John says is true. His own theory is that whites
need not fear blacks' acquiring money or power.
The blacks would use it for their own comfort, not
to control whites, as whites fear. The only hope he
sees is for blacks and whites to work together in
love for the good of the country. But Msimangu
fears that long before that happens, whites will
suffer the hatred of blacks for what they have done.
Embarrassed by so strong a speech, he says they'd
better hurry. Kumalo follows, weighted down with
new ideas.

The textile company can't help much, though
the men call in a worker who was friendly with
Absalom. This man, Dhlamini, says to try Mrs.
Ndlela at the edge of Sophiatown. She in turn directs them to Mrs. Mkize in Alexandra, but before
they leave Mrs. Ndlela, Msimangu pulls her aside
and asks why she looked at Kumalo with pity. She
says he looks like a good man, and she's sorry he
has a son she had to evict because she did not like
his friends.

The day nearly gone, the priests return to the
Mission House. Johannesburg hasn't made him
happy, Kumalo says, but he is enjoying Msimangu's company.

CHAPTER 8

The third day, the priests set off for the main
bus route, where every bus is the right one because they all go into Johannesburg. In the city,
more walking takes them to the buses for Alex-

andra, but they find a boycott underway to bring
the fare from 12 pence back down to 4. The leader
is the famous Dubula who seeks nothing for himself. Kumalo says his business is urgent and eleven
miles is a long walk, but Dubula points out that
people much older, and even the sick or the crip-
pled, walk that far every day.

Unwilling to disobey the boycott, the friends walk
for miles until at last a white man goes out of his
way to drive them through Johannesburg and beyond it to Alexandra—a poor black area so crime-
ridden that neighboring whites petitioned to have
it torn down. The petitions failed because the white
leader Professor Hoernle argued that it was one of
the few districts of Johannesburg where blacks could
own their homes. Still, old white women assaulted
for their purses near Alexandra have died, and even
white prostitutes sitting in cars have been attacked.

Their talking takes them to Mrs. Mkize's door,
but she hasn't seen Absalom for months. She acts
so frightened that Msimangu sends Kumalo to a
snack stall and questions her by himself. What does
this action suggest to you about Msimangu? Why
does Alan Paton show you that Msimangu knows
how to deal with people of all social classes in the
city? Yet even Msimangu has to swear not to talk
to the police before she will admit that Absalom
and his cousin brought stolen goods into her
house. Finally she gives a name, the taxi driver
Hlabeni. Hlabeni proves easy to find, but he too
fears the police and wants a guaranteed fare of 11
shillings before he will talk. He suggests a place
near Orlando where there are squatters. It's large,
but he says Msimangu can look up one of the so-

cial workers there. The readiness with which Msimangu accepts the suggestion again indicates that
he must have a wide circle of acquaintances in the
city.

Msimangu calls Kumalo over, and they take a
taxi home along the wide road that runs from Johannesburg to Pretoria. They see thousands of
people riding bicycles, thousands more walking
because of the boycott. Many whites are giving
rides. One white man is being harrassed by a policeman at a robot (traffic signal) for carrying black
passengers without a license. He is saying, "Then
take me to court." Kumalo is deeply moved at seeing
fellow blacks helped in public "by a white man,
for such a thing is not lightly done." Msimangu
marvels at the audacity of the words, "Take me to
court."

NOTE: Strict racial segregation existed in 1946,
even if it had not yet been codified by the government as apartheid. What comment can you make
about race problems in Johannesburg as illustrated
by this incident? Is it an oversimplification to say
that the problem can't merely be reduced to black
versus white? Are there people on both sides who
simply do what they consider right despite the
consequences?

CHAPTER 9

In this chapter—an intercalary chapter giving
background information—the narrator shows you
what is happening to blacks other than Kumalo in

Johannesburg. In a dozen short, dramatic scenes, we learn about the Shanty Town area near Orlando where Hlabeni has said Msimangu should take Kumalo next.

For both whites and blacks, it is true that "All roads lead to Johannesburg." But once they are there, blacks must go to slums like Alexandra and Orlando to rent a room or buy part of a house. If they pay enough they can get a room, but the house overflows. Quarrels break out and the evicted one makes the rounds again—but ten thousand others need homes, too. There's been war in Europe and North Africa, and no building is being done. A person can be on a list for months, even years like Mrs. Seme, with no guarantee of getting a place. Even bribery may not work. The young men in the crowded houses never seem to work or sleep, but they wear good clothing, white people's clothing. There will be trouble.

Finally, those who are desperate enough join Dubula's committee, and take him up on his idea. Everywhere in town there are discarded planks, tin cans, pieces of corrugated iron, old sacks. Overnight, thousands of families erect Shanty Town. As squatters they pay no rent, only a shilling to the committee. Children sicken and die without doctors, but people gather at night around the fires and sing "God Save Africa." White journalists take pictures. Other whites, wondering what "the poor devils" will do in winter rains, start building rough houses as Dubula said they would. Clearly, some whites have consciences, but there are limits. More squatters come, from Pimville and Alexandra and Sophiatown, but this time police drive them off.

CHAPTER 10

Kumalo plays with Gertrude's little boy while waiting to go to Shanty Town with Msimangu. He enjoys telling him about the beauty of Natal, until he remembers that now the hills are eroded and the earth is red and barren. Like philosophers and religious men from all eras of human history, Kumalo is struggling with the problem of evil. If God is good, why is it that people must suffer so much pain? Kumalo is somewhat like Job in the Bible, a good man who loses his belongings and even his children. Like him, Kumalo concludes that God's ways are mysterious and not to be questioned. Instead one should take joy in what one does have. But this answer has never satisfied social reformers, and even Msimangu has trouble with it, as you saw in Chapter 5.

Msimangu soon arrives, and takes Kumalo to Shanty Town. Some building is underway, and a few blacks are being allowed to train in white institutions as doctors and nurses. A nurse directs them to Mrs. Hlatshwayo, who says Absalom has been sent to the reformatory. Kumalo is crushed, though both he and Msimangu admit they've been expecting this. The priest from England, Father Vincent, has told Msimangu the reform school is a good place where boys who want to can change their ways. They begin their hour-long walk from Shanty Town into Orlando and on to the school.

NOTE: Paton draws heavily upon his own experiences as principal at Diepkloof for the school and the young white official whom Kumalo and Msimangu meet.

Msimangu and Kumalo arrive at the school at
noon, astonished at the number of boys there. A
pleasant black man takes them to a young white
official who speaks Afrikaans. Msimangu speaks
Afrikaans as well as Zulu and English, and Kumalo is embarrassed that he does not. The white
man says Kumalo may speak what he wishes. He
goes on to say that Absalom did so well at the
school that he has been released to marry a girl he
made pregnant. He has a job, and he's even saved
some money. Kumalo is stunned, but agrees the
real question is whether Absalom will lead a good
life from now on. After lunch the white man drives
them to Pimville, a village made out of storage
tanks cut in half as emergency housing only, but
still in use. He needs permission to enter, since
Pimville is for blacks only. He is perhaps even more
stunned than Msimangu and Kumalo to learn that
Absalom's girl hasn't seen him for days. The girl
herself, born and raised in Johannesburg, is de-
feated and doesn't seem to expect much of life.
Kumalo feels compassion for her, but Msimangu,
thinking he knows the type, angrily tells Kumalo
he can't even be sure the baby is Absalom's. And
even if it is, how many more are there? Does Kumalo plan to hunt up all of them? Deeply hurt,
Kumalo waits silently in the car. Meanwhile you
learn that Absalom hasn't been at work that week,
either. The white man is depressed, but says he
will continue the search, as he drops off the two
black priests where they can catch a train.

Msimangu, who has been silent, now begs Kumalo to forgive him for his sharp words. Why, in
your opinion, is Kumalo so quick to understand
and forgive his friend? He reminds Msimangu that
he himself said priests are but weak men whom

God has touched. Still, the fact that Msimangu and the reformatory official are so bitterly discouraged helps us realize there are no quick, easy answers to racial problems in Johannesburg.

CHAPTER 11

On the train back to Sophiatown, Msimangu asks Kumalo to join him two days later at Ezenzeleni, a settlement for the blind, where he can rest and pray and gain strength. The evening at the Mission House is pleasant until a white priest brings in the *Evening Star:* headlines report that three black youths have broken into the home of Arthur Jarvis and have killed him. The item reports that Arthur, a city engineer, fighter for justice, Anglican, and president of the African Boys' Club in Claremont, was the son of James Jarvis, the owner of High Place near Ndotsheni. Kumalo remembers Arthur as a cheerful boy who sometimes rode past St. Mark's. Arthur's wife, nine-year-old son, and five-year-old daughter were away on vacation, but he was home working on a paper on native crime when the crime occurred. "Cry, the beloved country," the narrator says; "these things are not yet at an end." It's the first time you've heard the title of the book used. Now you see that it contains the comma because its grammatical form is direct address to the land itself—the country should weep at how its inhabitants live.

Msimangu walks Kumalo to Mrs. Lithebe's. Kumalo is deathly afraid that Absalom was among the attackers. Msimangu tries to soothe him, but Kumalo feels beaten and old. Shock after shock has greeted him in Johannesburg, and now he feels he has no prayer left in him. Readers feel a grow-ing sense of disaster about to occur, and whatever their own beliefs, can sympathize with Kumalo. It would be for him the greatest loss of all if Johan-nesburg destroyed even his faith.

CHAPTER 12

In this chapter the omniscient narrator returns. Different styles of language strike your ears as you hear lyrical passages from the narrator alternated with quick, sharp, dramatic scenes being enacted in various parts of the city. Citizens in one white suburb want to hear a resolution demanding better police protection. Another man argues that more protection is only a temporary solution and that what is needed is better schooling. Others retort that schooling just produces more clever criminals. In another place, one man argues that it's unheal-thy to convict blacks who violate pass laws and send them to mix with real criminals. Society ma-trons argue the merits and practicality of recreation parks for blacks. Other people demand the com-plete cutting up of South Africa into black and white areas; still others say the compounds for male workers at mines and factories must be done away with so families can live together. The English-speaking churches call for education and oppor-tunity; the Afrikaans-speaking churches want to see the natives develop along their own paths, but do not define exactly what that means. In the end there is no agreement. Whites buy locks and dogs, and give up nighttime walks under the beautiful sky. The narrator says again, "Cry, the beloved country," because children yet unborn are better off. If they never learn to love their country, fear can't rob them of that love.

Next follows a series of short, dramatic scenes that telescope Kumalo's original search for Absalom into one day. Msimangu learns the police want Absalom. He sets off to retrace their steps, and Kumalo insists on going along and paying for the taxi. But the police, too, reached a dead end at the girl's door, and no one, not even the girl, knows exactly why the police want Absalom. How would you describe Kumalo at this point? Can you imagine the hope and the fear that must be tearing at his heart? No wonder his hands shake, back at the Mission House, as he pays the taxi driver. Things do not look good for Absalom, his only son whom he deeply loves.

CHAPTER 13

Thursday brings the trip to Ezenzeleni. The colony amazes Kumalo. English-speaking and Afrikaans-speaking whites actually work together to teach blind blacks how to make useful crafts. The white superintendent courteously leads Kumalo to a pleasant hillside, where he reflects for hours—especially about his son and Ndotsheni. Finally he accepts the fact that the old tribal ways are gone forever, but he also glimpses the possibility of building something new, through the schools. Then sadness again overwhelms him, until Msimangu preaches. Kumalo feels touched and healed, as if the beautiful words are for him alone. God will lead the blind by new ways, from darkness into light.

NOTE: Msimangu and the Barbarian Chief Msimangu differs from speakers mentioned so far—John Kumalo, Dubula, Tomlinson—because he combines a stirring voice with profound goodness. The government is relieved that he doesn't use his power to stir up rebellion, and some whites marvel that a man from the "barbarian tribe" that produced "the most terrible chief of all" can speak so beautifully. They mean the Zulu chief Dingaan, who led a massacre in the Kaffir Wars. The Boers, led by Pretorius, retaliated in a slaughter at Blood River on December 16, 1838. The date became "Dingaan's Day," a Boer holiday celebrating the triumph of "civilization over barbarism."

CHAPTER 14

The same day there is a great bustle at Mrs. Lithebe's. Buyers are carrying off Gertrude's decrepit furniture and fine aluminum pots and pans, while Kumalo prepares to play with his nephew. Then Msimangu and the young reformatory official appear, and the young man confirms Kumalo's worst fears. Absalom has been arrested for killing Arthur Jarvis, and John's son was one of the other boys. Kumalo cannot fathom what drives any man, much less his own son, to murder. He nods dumbly as the young man and Msimangu talk, and fumbles around him, not realizing he has already put on his coat and picked up his cane. Gertrude and Mrs. Lithebe wail with grief in the traditional way as Kumalo sets off for John's shop. He shuffles like someone very old or sick. For a moment, visualize this scene as if it were occurring in a film. The camera focuses closely on Kumalo's fumbling hands, staring eyes, and dragging feet. What do you conclude about his emotional state?

When Kumalo reaches his brother's shop, John doesn't notice these physical signs of distress. He jokes. Has Kumalo found the prodigal yet?

NOTE: The Parable of the Prodigal Son *Prodigal* means recklessly wasteful. A parable is a story about everyday people that ends with a moral. The parable of the prodigal appears in the Gospel according to Luke, Chapter 15. A rich farmer has two sons. The older one stays home and works hard, but the younger demands his inheritance, goes off to the city, and wastes it all in high living. His so-called friends disappear, and the prodigal soon considers himself lucky to get a job feeding pigs. When he notices that the pigs eat better than he does, he decides to go and apologize to his father, and ask if he may become merely a hired hand. He barely gets a chance to speak. His father is so happy that he kills a calf fattened for market and throws a huge party. The older brother is jealous, but the father explains that it's as if his brother has come back to life. The moral is that heaven rejoices when a sinner repents. John means Absalom by the prodigal, but it's interesting to think of John himself as a prodigal. Does it seem likely, though, that John will ever have a change of heart?

John's joking fades when Kumalo tells him Ab-

salom has been arrested for killing Arthur Jarvis.
John is afraid to ask about his own son, but Kumalo's silence conveys the message. John mur-
murs as Kumalo once did, "Tixo, Tixo." At the
mission Father Vincent takes Kumalo's hands and
offers to help, and the white man drives the Kumalos to the prison. John sees his son alone, but
the young white man goes with Kumalo. Like a
parent worried sick until a lost child turns up, Kumalo grows angry when he faces his boy at last.
He tortures both the boy and himself with questions that have no answers. Absalom did shoot
Arthur, but unintentionally, out of fear. Absalom
weeps, but maybe even he doesn't know whether
it's out of sorrow for himself, the girl, or the man
he killed, or simply out of frustration at being endlessly asked *why*.

Outside, John Kumalo is almost cheerful again.
He proposes hiring a lawyer who will lie. Kumalo
is stunned. How different John turns out to be
from the noble Dubula. In Kumalo's mind, John
will abandon family loyalty and truth itself for his
own benefit. Kumalo looks to the reformatory official for help, but that dedicated man is also so
bitterly upset that he offers only anger. He says
he's in the soul-saving business just like any priest,
and look what he gets. They leave separately, and
Kumalo remembers Father Vincent's offer.

CHAPTER 15

While Kumalo rests in his room before going to
Father Vincent, the young white man arrives. He
begs forgiveness for words said out of his own
grief, and urges Kumalo to find Absalom an hon-

est but capable lawyer. Together they go to the
Mission House, and Father Vincent promises not
only to find a lawyer, but also to look into per-
forming the marriage. When the young white man
has gone, the priests speak of all that has happened.

Kumalo uses a parable. A man is sleeping in the
grass while a great storm gathers overhead, and
everyone is afraid to wake him. Father Vincent
points out that the storm has broken; Kumalo's
fear is now replaced by sorrow. And if a storm
destroys a man's house, he can rebuild. Absalom's
amending his life must become more important to
Kumalo than his own sorrow. Kumalo does not
respond, so the younger priest orders him to pray
for justice and rebuilding, and even to give thanks
for the good things still in his life. He himself will
pray for Kumalo night and day. Of what importance is this help for Kumalo at this moment in his
life? Is it more important than getting a clever lawyer to defend his son?

CHAPTER 16

The next day Kumalo goes alone to Pimville to
see the girl. He tells her Absalom has killed a man,
and gives her the newspaper for the details. Then,
trying to find out her true nature, he begins a series
of questions like those he asked Gertrude and Absalom. The girl wants to please him, but she doesn't
know how. She hasn't had their moral training.
He taunts her cruelly with having had other criminal husbands, but never before a murderer. He
even traps her into saying she'd go to bed with
him if he insisted. Immediately more ashamed of

his own cruelty than her response, he apologizes sincerely. He knows her answer was only what she'd learned to say to survive. They talk more, and she shows interest in Ndotsheni. When he leaves she is smiling, and he feels as if a heavy weight has been slightly eased. He stops feeling guilty for actually having laughed a little when he thinks it may be due to Father Vincent's prayers.

CHAPTER 17

The point of view shifts to Mrs. Lithebe. She doesn't need to rent rooms, but is glad to have a priest in the house. She admires Kumalo for saving Gertrude, and it saddens her to see him so tragic-looking. She will not have him hurt further in her house. She readily agrees to take in the girl made pregnant by his son, and he gets her, using some of the last of his money from the cocoa tin. In what ways does Mrs. Lithebe find the girl to be different from Gertrude? Afraid that Gertrude may be leading the girl astray, Mrs. Lithebe carefully instructs her on proper behavior. The girl changes, and Gertrude finds her own amusement.

The point of view now shifts back to Kumalo, visiting the prison. The possible marriage and the hiring of a lawyer bring a spark of life to Absalom's eyes. Again Kumalo is tempted to be cruel and to force Absalom to admit the other two boys were never real friends. But this time compassion wins out. He holds his son's hands and gives him hope. As Kumalo leaves, the lawyer enters, and Kumalo meets him later at the Mission House. Mr. Carmichael is taking Absalom's case *pro deo* ("for God," that is, free). He would not defend clients who held to a lie, but he will defend Absalom. Still, he is not optimistic about the outcome.

Let's pause a moment to add up the clues that what has happened to Absalom is not just one family's problem, but a situation that summarizes racial issues in South Africa. In Chapter 14 you saw a white reformatory official grieving that his efforts had failed. You saw a black man abandon family and tribal loyalty to save his son, and a white priest violate the country's segregation code to take a black priest's hand in his own. In Chapter 15 you saw the same priest's willingness to use his white contacts to help blacks. In Chapter 16 you saw once more how conditions in Johannesburg undermine the moral sense of young blacks. And in this chapter you saw a white lawyer take a black youth's case for free. Clearly the issue is not just one murder committed by one young black, but flaws in a society that make such crimes almost inevitable and disturb blacks and whites alike.

BOOK II (CHAPTERS 18–29): TRIAL AND RECONCILIATION

CHAPTER 18

Book II opens word for word the same as Book I. But this time the scene stays on the rich uplands—High Place, the well-run farm of James Jarvis. Like Kumalo, Jarvis is a happily married man with a son he loves, a son who lives in Johannesburg. He is on the hilltop, thinking in a distant, uninvolved sort of way about the problems of erosion and lands reserved for blacks. The Afrikaner police he sees driving up the valley remind him of

how Afrikaner and English whites are now inter-
marrying—something unheard of in his father's day.
His wife Margaret meets the car, and sends Captain van Jaarsveld and Patrolman Binnendyk up
the hill. When they meet Jarvis on a small plateau,
van Jaarsveld breaks the news about Arthur. It's
the Tuesday the murder occurred; we've gone back
a few days in time. At the house Jarvis himself
tells Margaret, since she isn't physically strong.
The captain arranges a plane that will have the
Jarvises in Johannesburg by midnight.

CHAPTER 19

John Harrison meets the Jarvises at the airport.
He is Arthur's brother-in-law, the brother of Arthur's wife Mary.

NOTE: Names become a little confusing in this
chapter. "Harrison" refers not to John, but to his
father. "John" or "John Harrison" is used when
he is meant. "His daughter-in-law" is Jarvis's
daughter-in-law, Mary Harrison Jarvis.

John drives the Jarvises and Mary to the police
laboratories, telling them that no one in South Africa thought so deeply and clearly about "the native question" (racial problems) as Arthur. He stays
in the car while the others identify Arthur's body,
and then drives them back to the Harrison house.
Margaret goes upstairs with Mary, and the two
older men have a drink.
Harrison informs Jarvis of things he never knew

about his son. Messages have come from organi-
zations of every race. Arthur, who had by then
learned both Afrikaans and Zulu, had worked for
family camps instead of males-only compounds at
mines. He was outraged at conditions in hospitals
for non-whites. He had come to believe that black
crime was the fault of whites, and he and Mary
were willing to speak the truth as they saw it even
if it meant Arthur's job. All in all, Harrison says,
he was a kind of missionary. Jarvis' mind wanders
at the word "missionary," and he thinks of the
"dirty old" mission-church in Ndotsheni and its
"dirty old parson." With a shock, we realize he
means St. Mark's and Kumalo. Jarvis goes up to
bed and tells Margaret all Harrison has said. None
of it surprises her; she had always understood Arthur. Jarvis is sorry he had not.

CHAPTER 20

His wife and daughter-in-law leave Jarvis in his
son's house. There he is surrounded by books on
South Africa, U.S. President Abraham Lincoln,
justice, and religion, and portraits of two men who
died for their beliefs—Lincoln and Jesus. As Jarvis
glances through the heaps of books, papers, letters, and invitations, he is especially struck by all
the books about Lincoln, who was President during the Civil War, and by a quaintly phrased letter
from the Claremont African Boys' Club. He finds
and reads a fragment of one of Arthur's speeches.
It argues that exploitation of black labor is no longer
permissible, now that the cost is known in terms
of disintegration of black community life, poverty,
slums, and crime. Arthur argues that whites must

provide something to replace the old tribal system, which, with all its faults, was at least a moral system. Jarvis smokes his pipe and thinks for some time; then he reads Lincoln's Gettysburg Address and thinks again. Finally he takes the Lincoln book with him. The dark strain on the floor makes him think of Arthur as a small boy. He crosses it and passes the police guard at the door.

NOTE: The Jarvises, Alan Paton, and the Gettysburg Address Arthur's papers in this chapter and Chapters 21 and 24 come directly out of Alan Paton's own life and writing. Like Msimangu in Chapter 7, Arthur is a spokesman for the author. As for Jarvis, you are not told what he is thinking during long silences. You can only guess from what he says and does. Like Kumalo, he seems to be thinking about South African issues more deeply than ever before. You don't know why he finds the Gettysburg Address so meaningful, but these may be some lines that struck him: "It is for us the living rather to be dedicated here to the unfinished work which they who fought here have thus far so nobly advanced. . . .—that from these honored dead we take increased devotion to that cause for which they gave the last full measure of devotion—that we here highly resolve that these dead shall not have died in vain, that this nation under God shall have a new birth of freedom, and that government of the people, by the people, for the people shall not perish from the earth." Lincoln delivered the address in 1863, during the Civil War, at the dedication of a cemetery at Gettysburg battlefield. At the start of 1863 Lincoln had issued the

Emancipation Proclamation, which abolished slavery in the Confederate States.

CHAPTER 21

The funeral astonishes the Jarvises. People of different races come to honor Arthur, and it's the first time Jarvis has shaken hands with black people. The experience moves him deeply, and he begins to look at blacks as simply people like himself. After the funeral he has another talk with Harrison. He says he is sending Margaret, Mary, and the children back to High Place, but that he will stay to take care of Arthur's affairs. Harrison's reaction to Arthur's death is an indignant call for better police control of blacks. He then gets sidetracked to another issue, arguing that blacks have excellent treatment in mine compounds. Jarvis comments only that he wishes he could have heard Arthur argue with Harrison—a clue that Jarvis may not entirely agree with his host. When he turns to John Harrison to say he'd like to see that African Boys' Club in Claremont, John volunteers that he would be happy to take him. He had helped Arthur establish it.

The next morning Harrison tells Jarvis that the police have traced one of Arthur's attackers to Doornfontein Textiles, and have a lead on his friends. We are once again hearing about police work we've already followed—but this time from another father's point of view. After breakfast Jarvis picks up Arthur's manuscript on crime, the one he was working on when he was killed. If you've ever said "If only," you know the pain Jarvis feels when the wish passes through his mind that Arthur had never gone to investigate the noise. But he doesn't dwell on the past. Instead he reads the manuscript so he can better understand his son. He is deeply moved by Arthur's way of explaining that much of South African civilization is not truly Christian. The ideas send him again to the Lincoln book, and this time he reads the Second Inaugural Address. Again he sits, thinking and smoking his pipe. When Margaret comes, he gives her Arthur's manuscript, even though he knows that she, too, will dwell on the broken-off words, "Allow me a minute." Arthur never got that time.

NOTE: Lincoln's Second Inaugural Address   Again we don't know exactly which lines moved Jarvis. The following are the best known: "With malice toward none, with charity for all, with firmness in the right, as God gives us to see the right, let us strive on to finish the war [the Civil War] we are in, to bind up the nation's wounds, to care for him who shall have borne the battle and for his widow and his orphan—to do all which may achieve and cherish a just and lasting peace among ourselves and with all nations." You might want to review the famous speech yourself in order to determine what other sentences might have had an effect upon Jarvis.

CHAPTER 22

The omniscient narrator returns, describing the courtroom and, especially, the important role of the Judge. Judges justify the sentences they impose by quoting the law, which goes back to "the White People, for it is the White People that make the Law." The narrator's tone is somewhat sarcastic, implying that racial discrimination may be legal, but is it just? The trial itself, however, is a model of correctness.

Absalom Kumalo, Matthew Kumalo, and Johannes Pafuri are on trial for the murder of Arthur Trevelyan Jarvis on October 8, 1946. When Mr. Carmichael cannot get Absalom's charge changed from murder to culpable homicide, he has Absalom plead not guilty as the other boys have done. Absalom is quiet during the proceedings, but the other two act shocked at being accused of such things. Absalom is truthful on the stand, but we know it doesn't help his case when he can't explain why he had a bullet in the gun if he meant only to frighten people with it. At the end of the session everyone leaves, whites through their door and blacks through theirs. People point out James Jarvis, and Kumalo recognizes him as the man from the hills above Ndotsheni. Kumalo trembles. When murder itself horrifies him so deeply, how can he bear even to look at the father of the man his own son has killed?

CHAPTER 23

This chapter interrupts the trial to bring news of a rich gold discovery at Odendaalsrust in the Orange Free State. The structure of the chapter is like that of Chapter 12 inasmuch as it reports what many people are saying. But whereas in Chapter 12 the narrator spoke sadly of what fear was doing to the country, this time the narrator uses intense sarcasm to depict money-hungry whites as destroyers of the land. Read the chapter aloud, putting the sarcasm into your voice. Whom, in your opinion, are you encouraged to side with—the rich, or the "leftists" and "Kafferboeties"—those who work for the good of blacks? Praise is implied for Father Beresford, a courageous churchman who speaks out, and for Kafferboeties who say it's time to try out Sir Ernest Oppenheimer's idea for a new kind of mining camp—villages for whole families.

What is the point about how difficult it is to pronounce the Afrikaans "Odendaalsrust?" Compared with what is happening to blacks in Johannesburg, how does that concern for pronunciation strike you? Lest we miss the fact that we are to consider Johannesburg a terrible place, the narrator says what a good idea to build a new Johannesburg—why, it could even include another Shanty Town! Why might some readers consider this pure irony—words meaning exactly the opposite of what they appear to say? In the final two sentences, after the line of asterisks, the narrator ensures our understanding by dropping the irony to say, simply and straightforwardly, "No second Johannesburg is needed upon the earth. One is enough."

NOTE: The models for Father Beresford are Father Trevor Huddleston and Bishop Reeves of Johannesburg. During the 1960s, when Paton's passport was revoked, he was forbidden to see such outspoken Anglican friends of his as these two. Both were exiled from their country in the turmoil of the 1950s and early 1960s.

CHAPTER 24

Jarvis goes back to his son's house, again entering through the kitchen with its blood-stained floor. In Arthur's desk he finds a stack of neatly typewritten articles, and reads the one titled "Private Essay on the Evolution of a South African." Arthur says his childhood was wonderful and he learned honor and generosity, but the next lines shock Jarvis. He says his parents taught him nothing about the real issues in South Africa. It's hard for any father to be told by his son that he didn't think deeply enough, but imagine how it feels when the son has just died, in a way, for the beliefs he later held. Jarvis at first puts the paper down, but finds the strength of character to return and finish it. This time he is impressed at how passionately Arthur worked for justice for all South Africans, and at how he and Mary would have continued to do so whether or not their own children agreed with them.

Again Jarvis sits a long time, smoking and thinking. Then he leaves the house through the front door. The policeman thinks he's avoiding the bloodstain. Is that your opinion? How has Jarvis been affected by these events?

CHAPTER 25

One day when court is not in session the Jarvises visit a favorite niece of Margaret's, Barbara Smith, in the suburb of Springs. The women go shopping, and Jarvis starts to read the paper. Someone knocks on the back door, and he answers. It's an old parson whose collar is "brown with age or dirt." We realize it's Kumalo, on his errand for Sibeko, and it's definitely age, not dirt, that makes his collar look worn. After he greets Kumalo in Zulu, Jarvis is surprised when the parson trembles and sits down for some time, looking at the ground. He has trouble rising. Earlier Jarvis might barely have noticed expressions on the face of a Zulu, but by now he has changed enough to recognize that this man does not mean to be rude. He waits without complaining until Kumalo finally makes it to his feet, fumbles pathetically for the right piece of paper, and then asks about the daughter of Sibeko. Relieved, but finally getting a little irritated, Jarvis turns Kumalo over to a servant and goes back into the house.

Suddenly recognizing the old man as the parson from Ndotsheni, Jarvis comes out and says, "I know you, umfundisi." Considering how Kumalo felt about just looking at Jarvis in the courtroom, how do these words affect him? But Jarvis does not yet "know" this parson as having any connection with his son's killer. Still, he sees on Kumalo's face the suffering his words cause. He takes the initiative, telling Kumalo he can sit down. More talk makes him realize the parson is shaking not with illness but with fear, and he insists that the parson explain why. At last Kumalo gets the words out: "It was my son that killed your son." Once again we are given only Jarvis's actions and words, not his thoughts. He walks off, then comes back. He says, "I understand what I did not understand. There is no anger in me." He and Kumalo even talk about Arthur as a boy. Jarvis sees Kumalo's tears, and accepts his genuine sympathy for the entire Jarvis family.

Then Barbara Smith is back, and Jarvis explains Kumalo's errand in English. She says that the girl turned out bad, and she neither knows nor cares where she is. Not realizing at the moment that Kumalo understands English, Jarvis tells him, in Zulu, only the part about Barbara's not knowing where the girl is. What does his sensitivity in so small a thing tell you about his concern for Kumalo's feelings? Kumalo shows equal sensitivity. He could have embarrassed all three of them by saying goodbye in English. Instead he thanks Jarvis and his niece in Zulu. Jarvis watches awhile as Kumalo walks off, noticing how old the parson looks. Then he turns and sees that his wife, too, walks as if she were old.

NOTE: We've been told several times now, in different ways, that Margaret is frail. The repetition prepares us for events back in Ndotsheni in a later chapter.

CHAPTER 26

Back in Sophiatown, Johannesburg, John Kumalo is speaking. Dubula and Tomlinson envy him his powerful voice; policemen think the government ought to pick him up or shoot him; Kumalo is awed at how his brother's voice moves him. But Msimangu is glad the man is too corrupt to use his power fully. John urges higher wages but stops short of inciting a strike, lest he lose his own comfortable life. John Harrison and James Jarvis also listen, and then go on to John's and Arthur's boys' club.

Still, the strike occurs. The narrator says the miners include 300,000 black men from many areas within and outside South Africa. Worry that a strike might spread to all black laborers in the country proves groundless. The strike comes and goes, with no extension beyond the mines. Only three miners were killed in the fighting. (The narrator is again using a touch of sarcasm. The "only" would not have been used in news reports if the three dead men had been white owners instead of black workers.)

NOTE: In December, 1984, black South African Bishop Desmond Tutu complained that the whole world was upset over the murder of one Polish priest but few people were concerned over the daily killings of scores of blacks in South Africa.

A clergyman (Father Beresford, maybe?) at the annual meeting for priests attached to the diocese of Johannesburg says it's time to recognize the African Mine Workers' Union, but no one listens. The narrator again uses an ironic tone, wanting us to understand that those who link unions and tribal decay and lack of schools and crime are right, and that the quiet at the mines is like the apparent quiet in nature. In reality something is always stirring, and only fools think things are settled.

CHAPTER 27

The point of view shifts back to Mrs. Lithebe. She scolds Gertrude again, for seeing her former kind of companions, and tells her to leave Absalom's girl alone. A neighbor brings a newspaper with a headline about another white man killed by a black housebreaker, and Mrs. Lithebe and Msimangu worry that the event will affect Absalom's case. To keep Kumalo away from Mission House newspapers, Mrs. Lithebe invites Msimangu and Kumalo to eat with her and the young women that evening. After the meal they all attend a church meeting at which a black woman speaks about becoming a nun. Home again, Gertrude says that maybe becoming a nun would control her sexual desire, and that her brother's wife could then raise her child. Mrs. Lithebe is happy Gertrude has even had such a thought, but suggests she think about it further. On impulse, though, Gertrude tells the girl and receives from her two promises: to care for her son and to speak carelessly no longer.

CHAPTER 28

It is the day of sentencing, and an interpreter gives the Judge's words in Zulu so that all may understand. The Judge reviews the entire case. As you read, follow the judge's reasoning carefully. How would you have ruled if you were in his place? The judge says he is compelled to release Johannes and Matthew, although their previous criminal association will be investigated. As for Absalom, the judge admits the truth of Mr. Carmichael's arguments about the defects of society, but he must uphold the law. He sentences Absalom to death by hanging. Absalom falls to the floor sobbing, a woman wails, and an old man cries, "Tixo, Tixo." We know that has to have been Kumalo. The young white man and Msimangu are so grieved that together they ignore the color customs, both of them supporting Kumalo as they leave the courtroom.

CHAPTER 29

Father Vincent conducts the marriage ceremony at the prison. Msimangu, Gertrude, and the new wife leave, giving Kumalo and Absalom time to talk. Kumalo promises to raise the child to be born, and tells Absalom he and the girl are returning to Ndotsheni the next day. Absalom asks his father to do some errands for him, and then asks him to name his child Peter, if it is a boy. Absalom is terrified of hanging, and Kumalo comforts him. What a price they have had to pay to be reunited in love and understanding.

Back from the prison, Kumalo wants to know what John is going to do about his own son, lest Matthew end as Absalom has. John again refers to the parable of the prodigal son; he is determined to bring Matthew home and keep track of him. Kumalo then brings up the subject of politics, hoping to make John understand that he must not let hatred corrupt his use of his powerful voice. When John doesn't understand, Kumalo gets angry. Have you ever been so angry that your mouth seemed to blurt out words independently of your brain—words you were then unable to take back? If so, you can understand how anger and desperation lead Kumalo to tell John there's a spy in his shop. It could be true but isn't, so far as Kumalo knows, but he can't seem to undo his words. Then John says, "What a friend," and Kumalo can't help crying out that Absalom had two such friends. When John understands that Kumalo is talking about Matthew, he in turn is overwhelmed with anger, and kicks Kumalo out of his shop. Ashamed that he has spoken so differently from what he intended, but finding that John has already locked his door, Kumalo can only walk away. He knows he has lost his brother for good.

The Jarvises, too, are leaving. Harrison and Jarvis agree that the prosecutor should have hammered at Mrs. Mkize more in order to convict the two accomplices, but in a new understanding of how to prevent "native" crime, Jarvis also gives John Harrison a huge donation for the boys' club in Claremont.

There is a farewell party for the Kumalos that evening at Mrs. Lithebe's. Though Msimangu doesn't explain his motives, he reveals that he is to be the first black man in South Africa to enter a monastery, and everyone rejoices. At evening's end Kumalo walks Msimangu to the gate, and Msimangu gives him his savings. Kumalo weeps at having to leave his friend, and they promise to pray for one another. Back in his room, Kumalo opens the savings book to find that Msimangu has gifted him with more money than he's ever seen.

Before dawn the next morning, Kumalo wakes Absalom's wife and Gertrude's little boy, but Gertrude is gone. She has left behind the dress and turban he bought her, clothes for her new life. They have been discarded; Gertrude could not change after all. (Are you disappointed about Gertrude?) Kumalo has not succeeded in bringing back John and Matthew and Gertrude and Absalom. But he has, instead, a new family: a young girl, a little boy, and a child yet to be born.

BOOK III (CHAPTERS 30–36): REBUILDING

CHAPTER 30

The journey to Ndotsheni retraces the route Kumalo followed earlier. A catalog of names again suggests the distances and changing scenes. Near Ndotsheni the land is dry; rain is badly needed. People he knows start boarding the train, but Kumalo doesn't want to answer questions. Have you ever pretended to be sleeping, or read a magazine you didn't care about, to avoid talking? Kumalo's method is to read his sacred book.

Mrs. Kumalo and the man who carried the bags meet them. She welcomes her nephew and daughter-in-law as her own children, and all the villagers shower welcome on Kumalo as the family walks to Ndotsheni. They don't blame him for the actions of Gertrude and Absalom. The man who carries the bags says he works for Jarvis now, and that Margaret Jarvis is ill. Everyone joins in an impromptu service at the church, and Kumalo publicly asks God to forgive his sister and his son. The people kneel for his blessing. The new teacher suggests that they sing "God Save Africa," but aside from Kumalo, no one from Ndotsheni knows it yet. They don't have his vision. Kumalo and his friend talk of many things, including the daughter of Sibeko. Kumalo reports that Jarvis kindly left out the "I don't care" when he gave Barbara Smith's words in Zulu. Finally, Kumalo sits down with his wife. He gives her Msimangu's gift and then shares everything that has happened.

NOTE: The Sacred Book and the Blessing   Kumalo's "sacred book" may be a Bible or a breviary, a priest's book composed of daily prayers and Bible passages. Or it could be *The Book of Common Prayer*, the book of Anglican worship services. The first few words of the blessing come from Numbers 6; the second half is from 2 Corinthians 13.

CHAPTER 31

Kumalo prays for the restoration of Ndotsheni, but wants to do much more. He approaches the tribal chief and the school's headmaster, but they are powerless. Wondering whether his visions for the future were a delusion after all, he wearily works on the church accounts. He is interrupted by a small white boy on a red horse who does not seem to know about the usual stiffness between whites and blacks. They laugh together, especially when the boy practices his few words in Zulu. The boy grows serious, however, when Kumalo carefully explains why there is no milk for him—or even for sick black children who need it to get well.

That evening Kumalo's friend drives a cart full of milk cans to his door. Jarvis's grandson has asked him to send milk for the sick children. Speechless with joy, Kumalo doesn't seem to realize that the gift comes as much from his own courtesy to a small stranger as from the goodness of Jarvis. The friend goes off, so excited about driving the cart that he says his wife will think he has become a

magistrate (the judge in a local court). Kumalo
laughs heartily. His vision does not extend to black
men holding the same roles as whites in his society.

CHAPTER 32

Several letters arrive. Mr. Carmichael's letter says
that there will be no mercy. Kumalo and his wife
grieve, but she shakes it off faster. The one from
Absalom says that if he were at Ndotsheni, he
would never leave again. Msimangu reports the
Johannesburg news, and Kumalo is surprised
about his own nostalgia for that bewildering city.
Mrs. Kumalo departs with the letter from Absalom to his wife, and Kumalo goes out to study
the welcome rain clouds.

Standing there, he witnesses a strange ceremony involving the local magistrate, Jarvis, and
other white men with sticks and flags. The chief
rides up but obviously doesn't know what is going
on. The sticks and the box on the tripod are surveyors' instruments. Meanwhile it has been no ordinary storm building up. The white men leave
just in time, and after Jarvis turns his horse loose,
he joins Kumalo in the leaking church. They try to
stay dry during the deafening downpour. When
Jarvis asks Kumalo whether mercy was granted,
Kumalo shows him Carmichael's letter. Jarvis knows
what it is to lose a son, and tells Kumalo he understands. That evening Kumalo's people joke and
play around the surveyors' sticks until one of the
sticks is accidentally pulled up. They put it back
carefully, almost superstitiously, since they still
don't know what the sticks mean.

CHAPTER 33

Kumalo prays every day for the restoration of Ndotsheni, and a sick child gets well on the daily milk. One day the small white boy gallops up again, and again he and Kumalo enjoy a lighthearted conversation. Arthur need not have worried that his son might not be like him. Kumalo tells the boy that when he leaves, something bright will go out of Ndotsheni. The boy in turn compliments Mrs. Kumalo on her house. She is overcome at the realization that the son of the man Absalom killed has visited her house. After his Zulu lesson the boy leaves, passing a stranger who is near the church.

The stranger, a young black man, introduces himself as Napoleon Letsitsi, an agricultural demonstrator hired by Jarvis. Kumalo greets him as an "angel from God," and boards him in his own house. He has a pang of envy at learning Letsitsi earns more than he does, but rejoices that the young man really knows how to make the valley fruitful. Letsitsi also says the stakes mark a dam, which will prevent future droughts. A horse clatters up again; it is the small boy, come back to say goodbye. He is leaving the next day. And that, Kumalo says to Letsitsi, "is a small angel from God."

Kumalo's phrase puts into words something we can't help having felt in both Chapters 31 and 33. Arthur's son rides up to St. Mark's exactly as Arthur did in his boyhood, and, like Arthur, he seems so thoroughly good that he's too good to be true. In real life, the boy and Arthur would have flaws. But here, each of them is presented as a one-dimensional portrait to show us the best of Christianity in action.

CHAPTER 34

On another rain-threatening day, the Bishop is due for Confirmation services at St. Mark's. Before his arrival, Kumalo's friend comes home early in the empty cart. Jarvis has dismissed his workers because his wife has died. Kumalo feels unable to violate custom by visiting Jarvis in person, so he writes a short note expressing his and his people's grief. He worries whether he should even do that—what if Margaret died of grief? But his sympathy is real, and he sends a boy to High Place with the note.

Rain pours down during the confirmation service, so the celebration afterwards must be held in Kumalo's house. When the rain is finally over and the people have gone, the Bishop proposes transferring Kumalo to a parish far away from Jarvis. He is trying to be kind, but Kumalo is heartsick at the words. Then the boy he sent to High Place returns with a letter from Jarvis. In his letter, Jarvis thanks Kumalo for his note, and says that before she died, Margaret asked him to build a new church for the people of Ndotsheni. As if he had read Kumalo's mind, he adds that Margaret was sick before Arthur's death. In his joy Kumalo cries out, "This is from God!" What is the Bishop's tone when he asks to see this message from God? How does the Bishop behave after he has read it? Is there any question now of reassigning Kumalo?

Standing outside in the dark when the Bishop

has gone, Kumalo seems to hear a voice saying that God will comfort his people. The closeness to God that he felt himself losing in Johannesburg has returned completely. Going inside, he finds the women making a wreath for Margaret Jarvis. Kumalo's friend offers to go all the way to Carisbrooke to find the proper flowers, and Kumalo makes the card. They might have done this even before events in Johannesburg, but Jarvis is now far more likely to recognize the compassion the gift expresses.

CHAPTER 35

The action in this chapter is easy to summarize. But the issues recall for you the barren lands shown in the opening chapters of Books I and II, and the vision for change Kumalo had at Ezenzeleni. Consider, too, today's continuing unrest over land and rights issues in South Africa. As the chapter unfolds, whose *ideas* seem more realistic to you—Letsitsi's or Kumalo's? But whose *feelings* do you best understand? Why?

In this chapter, you see that agricultural progress is being made, but the people grumble. Why doesn't Letsitsi show gratitude to the whites who have educated him, or to Jarvis, who pays him? Why does he think that even if the land is restored, the reserves the whites have given blacks are too small for a growing population?

Kumalo feels too old to grapple with such views. If other blacks want to call him a white man's dog because he is grateful to Jarvis, fine. He has gone as far as he can.

CHAPTER 36

It's the fourteenth, and Absalom is to be executed the next dawn. As at other times of crisis in his life, Kumalo is going into the mountains to pray and keep watch, as Jesus sometimes did. Climbing, he meets Jarvis. They talk of the new church, Letsitsi's work, Jarvis' plans to live in Johannesburg, and how much the small boy resembles Arthur. Jarvis understands Kumalo's need to keep watch alone until his son has died. He indirectly tells Kumalo that good has come out of the crime. Until it happened, he was not aware of the greatness of the problems in South Africa. When he did become aware, he still didn't know what he could do. Instead of saying all that, however, all he says to Kumalo is that he was in darkness until they met. Neither man can fully break through the restrictions of a lifetime and tell the other everything he feels.

Kumalo begins his vigil by recalling his sins, especially the cruel lie to John which he was unable to correct. He prays for absolution, and then thanks God for the mysterious way his and Jarvis' pain is being transformed into gladness. He sleeps, and awakens at one in the morning, remembering why he is on the mountain. Like David who cried for his son, "O Absalom, my son, my son" (II Samuel 18:33), Kumalo too cries out, "My son, my son, my son." Again he sleeps, and wakes at four. He faces east and sets out the tea and maize cakes he brought along.

NOTE: The Sacrifice of a Son Kumalo's words and actions are those of the Anglican communion service. He may not be conscious of that, but it's appropriate—the communion service commemorates Jesus' offering himself for humanity. Kumalo's vigil and his willingness to let go of his son also parallel the willingness of Abraham to offer God his only son Isaac. That too occurred on a rock on a mountaintop. In Abraham's case, the son was spared. Isaac later had a son named Jacob who became the founder of an entire people, the twelve tribes of Israel (Genesis 22 and following chapters). Absalom is not spared, but his unborn child may be a son named Peter, and from Peter a new generation of South Africans may grow.

Kumalo takes off his hat as the sun rises. He has lost a son, and so has James Jarvis. But through their losses, they have been enlightened. Kumalo believes that more light will come to lead South Africa out of darkness. The mystery that remains is when the light will come.

A STEP BEYOND

Tests and Answers
TESTS

Test 1

1. *Cry, the Beloved Country*, is principally about _____
   - A. racial problems in South Africa
   - B. redemption from sin
   - C. crime and punishment in Johannesburg

2. The style of language most prominently _____
   used in this novel is based on
   - A. standard English vocabulary and rhythms
   - B. vocabulary and rhythms of the Afrikaans language
   - C. patterns from the Bible and Bantu languages

3. The event that most strongly focuses atten- _____
   tion on the crime problem among young blacks is
   - A. the making and selling of bad liquor in Claremont
   - B. the murder of Arthur Jarvis in Parkwold
   - C. an attack on a black girl in Sophiatown.

4. Which of these is a hopeful sign for im- _____
   provement of race relations?

    A. The lifting of racial restrictions in districts of Johannesburg

    B. White men erecting housing in Shanty Town

    C. The miners deciding not to strike at Odendaalsrust

5. What does Kumalo find most unusual about _____
the operation of the colony for the blind at Ezenzeleni?

    A. Afrikaans-speaking and English-speaking whites are working together

    B. White people are helping poor black people

    C. There are blind people among the black population

6. In this novel, more police and stricter con- _____
trol of the black population are most strongly urged by

    A. English-speaking liberals

    B. Afrikaner nationalists

    C. Zulu political speakers

7. Which of the following speakers combines _____
a stirring voice with profound goodness?

    A. John Kumalo   B. James Jarvis

    C. Msimangu

8. Which speaker does the government fear _____
because he arouses social action but seeks nothing for himself?

    A. Dubula   B. Msimangu

    C. John Kumalo

9. The decay of tribal life in the back country _____
is partially caused by

A. siphoning off of workers to white farms and mines
B. the attractions of the white men's cities
C. Both A. and B.

10. Why does John Harrison say, "when father _____ says Afrikaners he means Nationalists"?
   A. The Nationalist party includes English-speaking whites as well as Afrikaners
   B. John's father is not an Afrikaner, but has the attitudes he praises as being Afrikaner attitudes.
   C. Both A. and B.

Essay Questions

11. If Stephen Kumalo is the protagonist of this novel (the central character with the major conflict to resolve), then who or what is the antagonist (the person or force in his way)? Explain your reasoning.

12. Show that racial segregation in *Cry, the Beloved Country* is demonstrated by many daily customs as well as by such obvious things as separate buses and train coaches for Europeans and non-Europeans.

13. Explain in what sense Absalom Kumalo, Matthew Kumalo, and Arthur Jarvis could all be said to be victims of forces far greater than themselves and not of their own making.

14. The climax of a novel is defined as the point of highest dramatic intensity, or as the turning point in the plot. Defend either the murder of Arthur Jarvis or the trial and sentencing of Absalom Kumalo as the climax of *Cry, the Beloved Country*.

15. Defend or refute this statement: *Cry, the Beloved Country* is more a political statement than a novel.

Test 2

1. "There is a lovely road that runs from Ixopo   _____
   into the hills" is
   A. the opening sentence of Book I and
      Book II
   B. a line from Alan Paton's diary
   C. a line in a letter from James Jarvis to
      his son

2. The point of view used in *Cry, the Beloved*   _____
   Country is
   A. third person omniscient
   B. third person limited
   C. a combination of A. and B.

3. The man most dedicated to helping young   _____
   blacks leave crime and become useful citi-
   zens is
   A. the young white man from the reform
      school
   B. the white lawyer, Mr. Carmichael
   C. the black speaker and organizer,
      Dubula

4. Which of these is the strongest indication   _____
   of racial discrimination in South Africa?
   A. White drivers refusing to give rides to
      blacks during the bus boycott
   B. The training of black doctors and
      nurses in white institutions
   C. All laws being made by the white
      people

5. What does Jarvis find most unusual about _____
   the increase of Afrikaans-speaking whites
   in English-dominated Natal?
   A. Speakers of English and Afrikaans are
      marrying each other.
   B. Many of the Afrikaners speak English.
   C. Most of the government officials are
      Afrikaners.

6. Greater educational opportunities and bet- _____
   ter working conditions for natives are most
   strongly urged by
   A. John Harrison's father
   B. Arthur Jarvis
   C. Theophilus Msimangu

7. Which of the following speakers urges a _____
   good Christian life instead of pushing for
   political action?
   A. Msimangu   B. John Kumalo
   C. Dubula

8. The parent and child who change the most _____
   in the course of the novel are
   A. Gertrude and her son
   B. Stephen and Absalom Kumalo
   C. John and Matthew Kumalo

9. Restoration of the tribes in the rural areas _____
   requires
   A. an end to inefficient farming methods
   B. better education of black children
   C. both A. and B.

10. The woman in this novel who makes the _____
    greatest change in attitude is

    A. the girl who marries Absalom
    B. Gertrude Kumalo
    C. Stephen Kumalo's wife

Essay Questions

11. Explain in what sense *Cry, the Beloved Country* is a novel about fathers and sons.

12. Explain how the Kumalo family shows in miniature all the problems of blacks in South Africa.

13. Explain how the Jarvis family demonstrates the best of white attitudes in South Africa.

14. Show how the Reverend Theophilus Msimangu and Arthur Jarvis share some of the same beliefs and attitudes, and how they hold similar positions in their communities.

15. Defend this statement: *Cry, the Beloved Country* should be required reading for any ambassador to the Republic of South Africa.

ANSWERS

Test 1

1. A   2. C   3. B   4. B   5. A   6. B
7. C   8. A   9. C   10. C

11. Present some reasoning such as this, in your own words: To determine the antagonist it's necessary to know what the conflict is. In Book I, Kumalo struggles to locate his son, in Book II to achieve inner peace, and in Book III to do something for his people. It's difficult to see any one person in the story blocking his way. Instead, everywhere he turns, he runs into the deterioration of tribal ways, caused by the white men's intrusion in the

world of black Africans. The only antagonist that seems clear at all is the current socioeconomic situation for black Africans in Kumalo's world. This is shown by the laws of segregation, the wages paid black people, the lack of adequate housing, poor education and medical care for blacks, and the legal power held by whites. If any one group of people is the antagonist, it would have to be the white government. If the antagonist is a force, it has to be the whole weight of customs and traditions put into effect by whites and followed, almost without thinking, by everyone.

12. Specific examples will be particularly necessary in this answer, and the question excludes the most obvious ones. You might start with a sentence such as this to show that you grasp the question: Although restrictions on trains and buses clearly show apartheid at work, daily customs show it even more clearly. Then use examples that show how strongly both blacks and whites show that they know they must not be too friendly with each other. One example occurs at the Smiths' house when Jarvis doesn't help Kumalo get up, though he wants to, because a white man doesn't touch a black man. Or think of how Kumalo and Msimangu marvel at white men defying the law to carry blacks as passengers during the bus boycott. There are the forms of address, as well. Clearly it is a great honor for a white man to call Kumalo Mr. Kumalo instead of using the Zulu honorific umfundisi. Since the question doesn't mention the courtroom's being segregated, you might include that as well—a rather strong point, since the judge claims in his speech that justice is the same for all men, black or white.

13. In this answer you might borrow from your discussion of social pressures in answer 11. Absalom and Matthew might never have turned to crime had they been

able to earn a decent living and live in decent housing. Absalom in particular shows good character when in the reformatory setting; check what the white man in charge says of him in Chapter 10. Indeed, from his talks with his father, he seems to have fallen into crime more through fear of his companions than through his own inclinations. As for Arthur Jarvis, there would have been no need for him to die had not social pressures driven the Kumalo boys into a life of crime.

14. Whatever you defend as the climax, a place to start is the point of emotional intensity, the point at which you felt most strongly "Oh no!" or "I knew it!" Given the basic conflicts in this story, the turning point has to be considered the point at which Kumalo's search comes to an end and, also, the point which brings to a focus all the little bits and pieces presented up till then on the pressures causing blacks in Johannesburg to deteriorate morally. If the action has turned to tying up loose ends or the providing of solutions, we're past the climax. Both events named in the question certainly fit, but which fits better? Or could the actual moment of climax be yet a third event happening about that same time—the *arrest* of Absalom? Make your choice and then defend it according to the definition of climax.

15. To *defend* this statement you would want to stress chapters such as 9 (housing problems), 12 (arguments about native crime), and 23 (effects of the gold find at Odendaalsrust) which further the story very little, but which delve into social issues. You could also use the passages in various chapters where the omniscient narrator takes over and comments on tribal breakdown, the climate of fear in Johannesburg, etc. To *refute* the statement, you would want to stress the fact that all this information on social problems is presented through the fictional story of how all those pressures affect one black family and one white family. There would be no reason to discuss the social issues if it weren't for the Kumalos and the Jarvises—and their story is fiction.

Test 2

1. A   2. C   3. A   4. C   5. A   6. B
7. A   8. B   9. C   10. A

11. The fathers and sons involved are, of course, Stephen and Absalom Kumalo, John and Matthew Kumalo, and James and Arthur Jarvis. One way to respond is to show that there wouldn't be much story if the fathers did not have to face something that happened to sons they loved. Stephen Kumalo grows only through searching for, finding, and losing Absalom. John Kumalo doesn't change, but we would not have seen how shallow he is if we didn't see how he reacts to Matthew's arrest. James Jarvis would never have started to use his wealth to fight social problems if Arthur hadn't been killed. Another way to respond is to show ways all the fathers are alike (Anglicans, raised near Ixopo, love their sons, sons gone from home, etc.), and then show how all the sons are alike (involved with crime, hold views different from their fathers, etc.).

12. Two different approaches are possible here. You could start with members of the Kumalo family and list the problems encountered by each, or you could start by listing problems and then naming the family member whose life is touched by each. In any case, some of the points you might want to include are loss of religious faith (John, Gertrude), loss of the tradition of marital fidelity (John, Gertrude, Absalom's girl), crime caused by poverty and poor housing conditions (Gertrude, Absalom, Matthew), political oppression creating fear in black people (John, toward end of Book II), and so on.

13. You will want to cite the example of dedication shown by Arthur Jarvis' life, and also some of Arthur's beliefs from the middle chapters of Book II—Chapters 19 through 24, in particular. Your answer should also show what, specifically, James Jarvis does to begin to put Arthur's ideas into effect in Book III.

14. Msimangu's theories of social reform are presented in Chapter 7 after he and Kumalo talk with John Kumalo. Jarvis' theories appear most forcefully in his essay on the Christian dilemma in Chapter 21. Close reading of both sections will lead you to views the two men hold in common, such as the ultimate power being that of love of country and one's fellowmen, black or white. As for their standing in the community, the fact that Msimangu is highly regarded both by whites and blacks is shown by his effectiveness in obtaining information from factory managers and black people alike. According to the narrator in the chapter on Ezenzeleni, even the government is aware of Msimangu. The newspaper reports and the shocked reactions to Arthur's death easily make clear his standing in the white community.

15. The only reason anyone might dispute this statement is the book is set some time ago, in the mid 1940s. But roots of present problems always lie in the past, and this novel shows that racial problems in South Africa are not new. More important, the novel would enable the ambassador to experience a black African's point of view. Having read the novel, an ambassador who grasped its themes would be sure to go on to get a factual updating on the present situation as well.

Term Paper Ideas and Other Topics for Writing

The Novel

1. In what ways does *Cry, the Beloved Country* go beyond its South African setting to become a novel about problems fundamental to all human beings?

2. Could *Cry, the Beloved Country* be appreciated by someone who does not believe in God, in spite of the fact that most of its characters are Christians?

3. Compare the views on race relations in *Cry, the Beloved Country* with those offered by American black writers like Richard Wright (*Native Son*, 1940, *Black Boy*, 1945) and James Baldwin (*The Fire Next Time*, 1963).

4. What role do chance and coincidence play in *Cry, the Beloved Country*?

5. In what ways does the murder of Arthur Jarvis bring into focus all the social concerns of the novel?

Literary Topics

1. What are the various literary definitions of tragedy and how do they apply to *Cry, the Beloved Country*?

2. In what ways do beliefs, language, and phrasing provide clues to the characters' ethnic groups? Give several examples for each ethnic group represented.

3. Locate a copy of Maxwell Anderson's script for the 1949 musical play *Lost in the Stars*, based on *Cry, the Beloved Country*. Compare the play with the novel. What does the musical version add to or detract from the novel?

Themes, Symbols, Biblical Parallels

1. What is the significance of Arthur Jarvis' interest in Abraham Lincoln, particularly Lincoln's Gettysburg Address?

2. Trace the themes of confession, repentance, and forgiveness through the novel.

3. In what ways does the Biblical story of King David and Absalom parallel or differ from that of Kumalo and his son? Include the father-son relationship, what becomes of each Absalom, and how each father reacts.

4. Apply the parable of the prodigal son from the Gospel according to Luke to various members of the Kumalo family—Absalom, John, Matthew.

5. Is Arthur Jarvis a Christ figure?

6. Discuss the themes of light and darkness, sight and blindness, and the coming of dawn in the novel.

Characters

1. In what ways do Msimangu, Arthur Jarvis, and the young white man from the reformatory reflect the life and opinions of Alan Paton?

2. What was the judge's reasoning in reaching his verdict on Absalom Kumalo, Matthew Kumalo, and Johannes Pafuri? Would you have reached the same conclusion? Explain and defend your answer.

3. In what ways are Stephen Kumalo, John Kumalo, and James Jarvis alike? In what ways are they different? How does Paton use their similarities and differences?

Social Issues

1. What is the role of women in the novel? Are they presented as men's inferiors, superiors, or equals?

2. Cite at least three examples of social protest in the novel. In each case, include both cause and outcome, and whether or not you consider the protest justified.

3. In what ways has the situation in South Africa changed since Paton wrote *Cry, the Beloved Country?* Are nonwhites better or worse off now? Has the novel had any effect on South Africa's government?

Further Reading
WORKS ON SOUTH AFRICA

Argyle, J. and E. Preston-Whyte (eds.). *Social System and Traditions in South Africa.* Cape Town: Oxford University Press, 1978.

Carter, Gwendolen. *Which Way is South Africa Going?* Bloomington: Indiana University Press, 1980.

de Kiewiet, C. W. *A History of South Africa, Social and Economic.* London: Oxford University Press, 1957.

Hoagland, Jim. *South Africa—Civilizations in Conflict.* Boston: Houghton Mifflin, 1972.

Kiley, Dennis. *South Africa.* London: B. T. Batsford Ltd., 1976.

Moodie, T. Dunbar. *The Rise of Afrikanerdom: Power, Apartheid and the Afrikaner Civil Religion.* Berkeley: University of California Press, 1975.

CRITICAL WORKS

Baker, Sheridan, ed. *Paton's Cry, the Beloved Country: The Novel, The Critics, The Setting.* New York: Charles Scribner's Sons, 1968.

Baker, Sheridan. "Paton's Beloved Country and the Morality of Geography," *College English,* XIX, October, 1957, pages 56–61.

Callan, Edward. *Alan Paton*. New York: Twayne Publishers, 1968. Biography and analysis of Paton's work.

Sussman, Andrew. "Three Writers." *Publishers Weekly*, 21(April, 23 1982). Comments from Paton on publishing and censorship in South Africa today.

ADAPTATIONS OF *CRY, THE BELOVED COUNTRY*

Anderson, Maxwell. *Lost in the Stars: The Dramatization of Alan Paton's Novel*. New York: W. Sloane Associates, 1950.

Komai, Felicia, with Josephine Douglas. *Cry, the Beloved Country: A Verse Drama*. New York: Friendship Press, 1955.

AUTHOR'S OTHER WORKS

1953 *Too Late the Phalarope*. A novel with Afrikaner main characters.

1955 *The Land and People of South Africa*. Written for high school students. (Revised ed., 1972.)

1956 *South Africa in Transition*. With Dan Weiner. Essays.

1958 *Hope for South Africa*. Historical analysis of South Africa's cultural and racial problems.

1960 *Mkhumbane*. A play, "Village in the Gulley," written for a mixed-race cast in Durban, South Africa.

1961 *Tales from a Troubled Land* (English edition, *Debbie Go Home*). Ten short stories including "Debbie Go Home" and "Sponono."

1965 *South African Tragedy* (South African edition, *Hofmeyr*). The life and times of Jan Hendrik Hofmeyr.

1965 *Sponono*. With Krishna Shah. A play about a boy from Diepkloof.

1968 *Instrument of Thy Peace*. Meditations based on the
writing of St. Francis.

1968 *The Long View*. Edited by Edward Callan. Paton's
essays in the Liberal periodical *Contact, 1958–1966*.

1969 *For You Departed*. A memoir and tribute to Paton's
first wife.

1973 *Apartheid and the Archbishop*. The life and times of
Geoffrey Clayton, Archbishop of Cape Town.

1975 *Knocking on the Door*. Shorter writings selected and
edited by Colin Gardner.

1980 *Towards the Mountains*. Autobiography to 1948.

1981 *Ah, But Your Land Is Beautiful*. Novel set amid events
of the early 1950s in South Africa.

GLOSSARY

This glossary includes many place names, as well
as Zulu, Xhosa, and Afrikaans words used in *Cry,
the Beloved Country*. Pronunciations are given only
for words that do not follow the regular rules of
English pronunciation.

Afrikaans   (af-ri-KANZ) A language also called Cape
Dutch or South African Dutch, developed from Dutch
spoken by 17th-century European settlers. Both Afrikaans and English are official languages of South
Africa.

Afrikaner   (af-ri-KAHN-er) A white, Afrikaans-speaking descendant of early European settlers.

Alexandra   A crime-ridden suburb of Johannesburg
where blacks could own land.

Apartheid   (a-PAR-tade) Afrikaans for "separation" or
"apartness." An official government policy of separation of the races.

Bantu Blacks in South Africa or the languages they speak.

Basutoland See Lesotho in this glossary.

Boer (BO-er, BU-er) Afrikaans for "farmer." Originally applied to settlers of Dutch descent but broadened to include all Afrikaans-speaking European settlers.

Coloureds People of mixed race.

Donga A steep riverbank.

Drakensberg Literally, dragon (drakens) mountains (berg). An extensive mountain range in eastern South Africa

Europeans White people.

Ingeli (in-GAY-lee) A place near Ixopo.

Inkosana (in-ko-SAHN) Zulu, little chief or little master.

Inkosi (in-KOSE) Zulu for chief or master.

Inkosikazi (in-KOSE-e-gahz) Zulu for mistress.

Ixopo (ik-OH-po) A village in Natal.

Johannesburg The largest city of South Africa, established in 1886 by gold miners.

Kafferboetie (*boetie* rhymes with *goody*: KAF-er-boody) A white who works for the good of nonwhites. Literally, "little brother of the Kaffir." Originally an Afrikaans term of comtempt.

Kaffir, Kaffer Afrikaans for infidel of heathen. An insulting term applied to black Africans.

Kloof A deep ravine or a valley with steep sides.

Kraal (CRAWL) A village made up of a collection of huts surrounded by a stockade, or an enclosure for livestock.

Lesotho A kingdom called Basutoland before independence in 1966. It lies near the Drakensberg Mountains and is entirely surrounded by South Africa.

Lobola A black African custom of buying a wife with cattle.

Lorry Truck.

Natal (na-TALL) An eastern province of South Africa lying between the Drakensberg Mountains and the Indian Ocean.

Nationalist Member of an Afrikaner-dominated political party that favors racial segregation.

Native, Native African A black African.

Ndotsheni (in-dot-SHAY-nee) A Zulu village in Natal.

Nikosi sikelel' iAfrica (in-KO-see see-gay-LELL ee-AH-frekah) Slogan and song, "God Save Africa."

Non-Europeans Nonwhites: Asians, Coloureds, and blacks.

Odendaalsrust (oh-den-dolls-ROOST) Site of an April 1946 gold strike in the Orange Free State.

Orange Free State A province of South Africa bounded by the Orange and Vaal rivers. At one time it was an independent Boer republic.

Orlando A Johannesburg district adjacent to Shanty Town.

Petrol station Gasoline station.

Pietermaritzburg (pe-ter-MAR-itz-burg) Capital of the province of Natal.

Pimville A black district of Johannesburg with dwellings made of storage tanks cut in half. Originally intended as emergency housing only.

Pounds, shillings, pence South African currency before 1961. One pound contained 20 shillings or 240 pence (pennies). At 1946 exchange rates, 1 South African pound was equivalent to $4.03 in U.S. dollars, 1 shilling equivalent to 20 cents, and 1 penny equivalent to 1.6 cent.

Pretoria Capital of Transvaal. In *Cry, the Beloved Country*, "Going to Pretoria" means going to be executed.

Shanty Town A Johannesburg slum built up overnight out of scraps by black people desperate for housing.

Siyafa (see-YAW-fa) A fatalistic expression, "We die."

Sophiatown (so-FEE-a-town) A mixed-race district of Johannesburg where blacks could own property.

Titihoya (tit-ee-HOY-a) A bird similar to a plover. The name imitates the sound the bird makes.

Tixo (TEE-ko) Xhosa for Great Spirit, God.

Transvaal (trahns-VALL) A northeastern province of South Africa, at one time an independent Boer republic.

Umfundisi (oom-FOON-dees) A Zulu title of respect.

Umkomaas (oom-KO-mahs) A river and valley in Natal.

Umnumzana (oom-NOOM-zahn) Zulu for Sir.

Umzimkulu (oom-zim-KOO-loo) A river and valley in Natal.

uSmith, uJarvis Zulu equivalents of Mr. Smith, Mr. Jarvis.

Veld, veldt (FELT) Grassland with scattered shrubs or trees. *The Veldt* means the great central plateau on which Johannesburg is located.

Xhosa, Xosa (KO-sa) A Bantu-speaking people of eastern and central South Africa.

Zulu A Bantu-speaking people of the Natal area.

The Critics

Alan Paton

Alan Paton. . .needs no introduction to Americans. "Cry, the Beloved Country" was published in 1948, and ever since he has been cited as one of the premier South African writers of his time: perhaps of all time. . . . He is 78 years old now and his voice is slow and deliberate, but the words offer years of careful thought. He has lived through changes in government, people and publishing, and witnessed the economic growth of his nation. And, perhaps more than any other living South African author, he has chronicled these changes for the world to read.

Andrew Sussman, "Three Writers," *Publishers Weekly*, 1982

The Novel

Cry, the Beloved Country may be longer remembered than any other novel of 1948, but not because it fits into any pattern of the modern novel. It stands by itself; it creates rather than follows a tradition. It is at once unashamedly innocent and subtly sophisticated. It is a story; it is a prophecy; it is a psalm. It is passionately African, as no book before it had been; it is universal.

Lewis Gannett, "Introduction," *Cry, the Beloved Country*, 1948

Injustice Shown without Violence

Cry, the Beloved Country is a great novel, but not because it speaks out against racial intolerance and its bitter effects. Rather the haunting milieu of a civilization choking out its own vitality is evoked naturally and summons our compassion. There are no brutal invectives, no blatant injustices to sear the reader's conscience, no vicious hatred, no righteously unleashed passon. It is a great compliment to Paton's genius that he communicates both a story and a lasting impression without bristling, bitter anger.

F. Charles Rooney, "The 'Message' of Alan Paton," *Catholic World*, 1961, in *Paton's Cry, the Beloved Country: The Novel, The Critics, The Setting*, ed. Sheridan Baker, 1968

Stephen Kumalo

The mainspring of this unusual book is saintliness. The hero, an old Zulu minister, the Reverend Ste-

phen Kumalo, is a feat of characterization rare in
the modern novel: a convincing portrait of a saintly
man.

> Charles J. Rolo, "Reader's
> Choice," *The Atlantic Monthly*,
> 1948, in *Paton's Cry, the Beloved
> Country: The Novel, The Critics, The
> Setting*, ed. Sheridan Baker, 1968

Theme of the Novel

Paton succeeds to a remarkable degree in portraying
a segment of South African life during a brief period
immediately following the end of World War II. And
he succeeds, to an even more remarkable degree,
in endowing this regional portrait with universal
significance. He accomplishes this by incorporating
into the actualities of South Africa's physical and
social setting a fundamental theme of social disintegration and moral restoration. This theme is worked
out through two complementary, or counter-
pointed, actions: Stephen Kumalo's physcial search
for his son Absalom, and James Jarvis' intellectual
search for the spirit of his son Arthur. In each case,
the journey, once undertaken, leads to an inner,
spiritual awakening.

> Edward Callan, *Alan Paton*, 1968

Style of Language

[There is] a dominant style associated with the book.
This is the pattern of speech with a marked poetic
quality accorded to Kumalo and the African characters generally, and also to some extent employed
in the lyric passages voiced from outside the action.
This quality can be viewed as an artistic re-creation,
in English, of the sound and syntax of spoken Zulu.
But to be more precise, it is an artistic amalgam: a
melting-pot of African and other speech patterns
analogous to the tribal melting-pot in industrial Johannesburg. Thus, the language of *Cry, the Beloved
Country* is a poetic invention designed to carry over
into English the effects of the sound and idiom of
African speech.

At least as many readers were drawn to *Cry, the Beloved Country* by the freshness of its language and the pleasure of its rhythms as by its insights into social dilemmas and complex relations among races. In contrast to the commonplace language of journalism they found Paton's language fresh and lively.

Edward Callan, *Alan Paton*, 1968

NOTES

NOTES